THE 1935 REPUBLICAN RIVER FLOOD

THE 1935 REPUBLICAN RIVER FLOOD

JOY HAYDEN

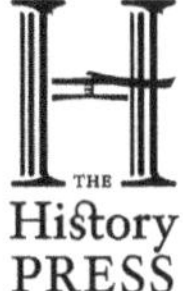

Published by The History Press
Charleston, SC 29403
www.historypress.net

Front cover: photo by Don Gibson, courtesy of the Museum of the High Plains, McCook, Nebraska.
Back cover, top: Joseph Torrey. *Bottom*: Cheyenne County Museum, St. Francis, Kansas.

First published 2015

Manufactured in the United States

ISBN 978.1.62619.855.5

Library of Congress Control Number: 2014956403

Farmers and villagers say that after the drought come two other dreaded Riders of the Apocalypse—flood and tornado.
—McCook Daily Gazette, *June 3, 1935*

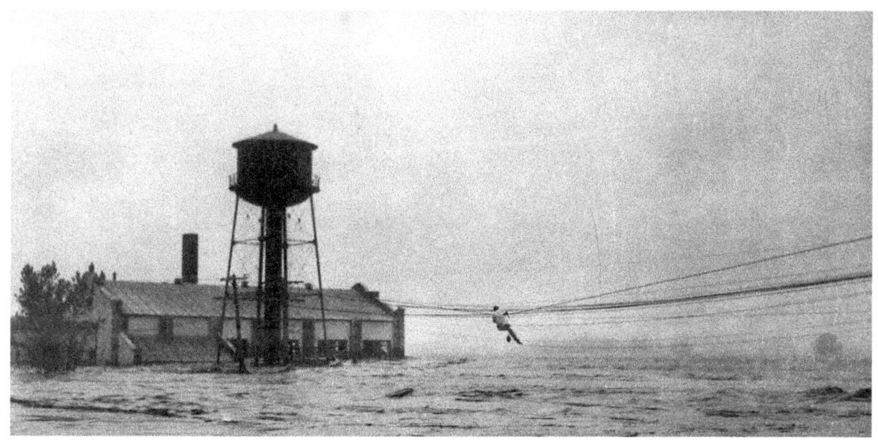

An attempt to rescue men trapped at the McCook Power Plant. *Don Gibson.*

This book is dedicated to all those who lost their lives during the 1935 Republican River flood.

Contents

ACKNOWLEDGEMENTS

I became interested in the 1935 Republican River flood about a year before the seventy-fifth anniversary of the event in 2010. I spent many hours researching the flood in communities all along the river. I discovered that while several self-published books had been written, no recent account of the flood told the story from its beginning in Colorado and Kansas through its rampage in Nebraska to its final end in Kansas. I was fortunate to visit with many survivors—some of whom have since passed away—who provided firsthand information about the event all along the river.

Marlene Harvey Wilmot provided a treasure-trove of information about the flood. If not for her efforts to document the flood, recount the memories of her father's heroism and tell the stories of countless others who lived through the flood, most of their stories would never have been recorded. I have, with her permission, drawn extensively from her work and our conversations in the description of events recorded in these pages.

Special thanks to Lucille Edwards, Nancy McKenzie, Mary Sherk and Joseph Torrey, who lent me their photographs, many of which illustrate this volume. Mr. Torrey's photos were from a collection he preserved taken by a local photographer named Webber, who photographed the flood in Alma, Naponee and Orleans, Nebraska. I am also deeply grateful to the many museums and historical societies along the river that so generously shared their knowledge of the flood and the stories and photos they had collected over the years. The Cheyenne County (Kansas) Museum and the Museum of the High Plains in McCook, Nebraska, shared both photographs and stories that were particularly helpful in piecing together the story of the flood.

I am deeply grateful to Scott Mentzer, Meteorologist in Charge, at the National Weather Service in Goodland, Kansas, who encouraged me to write this book and read through the many changes in the manuscript along the way to publication. The staff at the National Weather Service in Goodland, Kansas, not only provided detailed weather information about the event but also created an excellent 1935 Republican River Flood webpage with many more details about the weather conditions before, during and after the flood. This website is a treasure for anyone interested in knowing more about this event.

Many other contributors are listed in the back of this book. Although it is impossible to name all the people who helped in the making of this book, please know that although your name might not be mentioned, I appreciated all the help given me in preparing this manuscript. I regret any mistakes that might have occurred while collecting and transcribing the stories of the flood. Whether you shared your story, provided a picture for the photo collection or provided newspapers or other documents, I am deeply grateful for your help in telling this story.

Introduction

My God, save my babies!" As the section of the roof on which she stood collapsed into frigid floodwaters, Frances Miller screamed these haunting words. Dale Miller, Frances's brother-in-law, watched in horror from another section of the roof only a few feet away. He tossed his nephew Johnny into a tree. Clutching his niece, Nadine, he plunged into the debris-filled water and fought to make it to shore.

Meanwhile, Frances's husband, Charles Miller, lay in town seriously ill. Frances had heard news of approaching high water earlier that day and chose to keep their six children at home on their farm near McCook, Nebraska, since they were also ill. She did not worry much about a flood. There were so many other things to worry about; the terrible drought and the struggle she and Charles had making a living for the family from day to day were more than enough to keep her occupied. She knew the Republican rose often in the spring, and it was more a nuisance than a danger most years. As dry as it had been for so many years, it was hard to believe there could be a flood.

Frances did not see the ten-foot wall of water headed for their house. She did not know that, within hours, her farm would be covered by a roaring river intent on taking the lives of all who huddled in her home. Those in her house that day included her children: Claudine; Charles Frances, called "Johnny"; Charlotte; Nadine; Virginia Mae; and Beverly, a tiny infant. Others adults in the house included Elizabeth Shook, Frances's sister, who worked as a local schoolteacher; Fred Swanson; and Nels Nielson. Both men had taken shelter in her home after having been caught by surprise by the rising river as they checked on their cattle in the area.

Dale Miller, her brother-in-law, a father with five children of his own, realized the danger his brother's family faced when he saw the flood approaching McCook. He tried to think of a way to reach them. He hurried to the home of Clyde McKellip and asked to borrow his boat. Clyde did not know the Miller family well but decided impulsively to help Dale rescue his brother's family.

The two men rowed the small boat to the Miller house. They could see it being rapidly surrounded by rising water as they approached. They realized the broken oarlock on the boat made it useless for rescuing a large number of people in the flood, now coming in ever-rising waves. The men reached the house just as the water started coming inside.

Swanson, unable to swim, panicked and jumped into the damaged boat Dale and Clyde left tethered outside. It capsized, and he went under, screaming in terror while those trapped in the house watched in horror. Nielson also abandoned the group and swam outside to the dairy barn. He climbed on the roof just before the river tore it from its foundation and began to move the structure downstream.

Meanwhile, water poured in the windows of the house. Summoning strength he did not know he possessed, Dale stood on the bed in a back bedroom and broke through the ceiling to the attic. Clyde handed the children up to him, followed by Frances and Elizabeth. Elizabeth kept her purse with her, with her last paycheck from teaching school tucked carefully inside. Dale chopped another hole through the roof, and they all climbed outside.

Within twelve minutes, the water had risen ten feet. The house began to move, torn from its foundation by the angry river. The adults vowed they would each hold on to one of the younger children if the house started to collapse under their feet. As they were talking, the house moved again, and the river slammed the house and barn together, tossing everyone into the churning water.

Clyde held Charlotte and tried to hold on to Frances, but she slipped from his grasp. Frances lost her grip on baby Beverly. Clyde caught the baby, but the river tore the child from his free hand. Frances and Beverly slipped beneath the fetid water. Clyde reached a tree and managed to find a perch so he could sit and hold Charlotte. They remained there, prisoners of the flood for almost twenty-four hours.

Dale and Nadine were tossed from tree to tree as the river toyed with them. It battered them with debris as Dale clung to the child and fought to keep their heads above water. Finally, he found a tree sturdy enough to hold their weight. The sky grew as dark as night, and they held on tight while a tornado passed over them. Buffeted by the cold wind and icy rain, Dale held fast to the tree as Nadine clung to him. The tree served as their home throughout the chilly night.

The next morning, airplanes searched for survivors. Even though Dale removed his shirt and waved it at a plane that passed directly overhead, the aircraft flew by without seeing the pair. The river was still high and running fast, but Dale decided the time had come to swim to safety. Placing Nadine on his back, he swam to a nearby sandbar. They remained there for a time while Dale rested. Nearing exhaustion, he decided to set out again, this time to go for help. Realizing he could make the riverbank much faster by leaving Nadine, he dug a little pit in the sand to protect her. He threatened her with a spanking if she moved from the spot and then struck out to reach the riverbank and the nearest farmhouse.

The woman who answered his knock discovered a wild-eyed man covered in mud, with his face and hands unrecognizable from the terrible beating inflicted on him by the debris-packed river. His entire body was also swollen and blistered from exposure and sunburn. Dale tried to talk, but his dry throat prevented speech. Seeing his struggle to talk, the frightened woman offered him a cup of warm water. Refreshed, he managed to tell her about Nadine. The woman ran to find help for Dale and his niece.

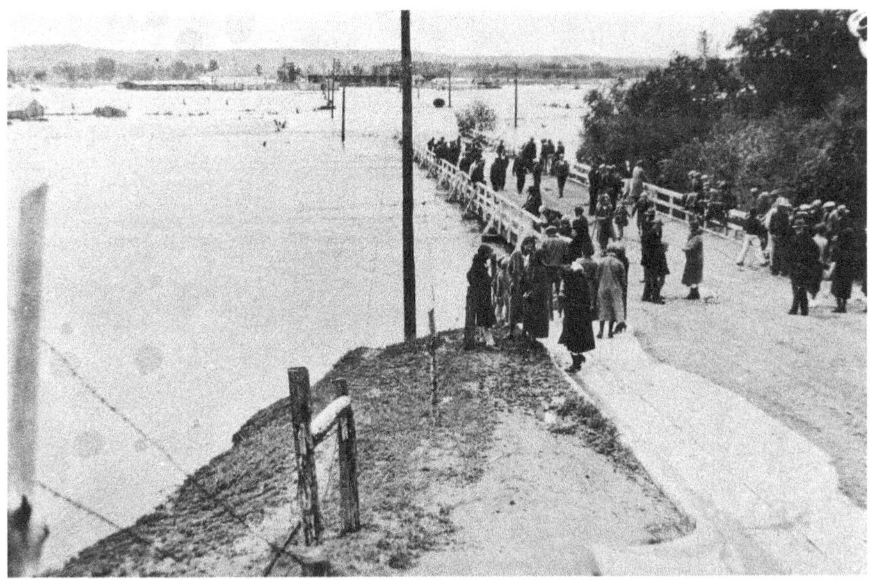

A flooded bridge near McCook, Nebraska. *Museum of the High Plains.*

Neighbors soon flocked to take care of Dale. They followed his instructions and found Nadine waiting on the sandbar. Although she protested that she would get a spanking if she moved, her rescuers convinced her to come with them and reunited her with Dale. Both soon joined family waiting in McCook. Sadly, only Nadine and Charlotte were returned to their father. The river wiped out the rest of his family.

Along with more than one hundred other people, the drowned members of the Miller family were victims of the 1935 Republican River flood. This flood remains the greatest in recorded history in the tri-state area of Colorado, Kansas and Nebraska. Local historians agree that it is the deadliest weather event of any kind to occur in the Republican River Valley in modern history.

The flood changed the land it passed over forever. The torrential rain and the resulting flood altered the land, moved the river channel and forced changes on the people who lived nearby. Understanding the flood and the transformation it brought to the area are important both to comprehend the events of the past and to prepare for any similar events in the future.

In 1935, the Great Plains were reeling from the blows inflicted by two disasters. Severe drought in the Republican River Valley left people searching for water. The second disaster had started in a far-off place called Wall Street six years earlier. When the stock market crashed, the hopes and dreams of those in the Republican River Valley plummeted right along with it and plunged both the regional and national economy into the Great Depression.

Both events resulted in hard times for people trying to make a living in the Republican Valley of Kansas, Colorado and Nebraska. The High Plains sweltered and dried to dust. Scoured by dust storms that came with withering regularity, any hope of a good crop or healthy livestock became an impossible dream.

Plagues of grasshoppers, tornadoes and seemingly ceaseless wind tormented the region. Dust storms grew so powerful that High Plains dirt clouded the air even as far away as Washington, D.C. On March 21, 1935, the *Stratton News* in Nebraska reported that sixty- to seventy-mile-per-hour winds filled snow fences along the highway with mounds of dirt. The paper added that daylight turned to night when streetlights failed to give any relief from the blinding clouds of windborne dust.

A few years earlier, on March 30, 1930, Herbert Hoover had announced that the worst of the deplorable conditions were over, but in the Republican River Valley, the worst was yet to come. Dirt smothered crops and buried the hopes of those living in rural communities. Unlike relatives and friends in the more populated areas of Omaha, Kansas City or Denver, residents of the rural portions of Kansas, Colorado and Nebraska had no soup kitchens, no bread lines and little relief from the grinding poverty gripping the nation.

Like other parts of the country, unemployment rose as high as 25 percent, with entire families looking for work. The merciless drought compelled the governor of Colorado, Ed Johnson, to issue a proclamation designating May 22, 1935, as a day of prayer in Colorado. He urged all citizens to pray for rain to relieve the "dust storms, erosion, devastation, sickness, discouragement and want" that plagued his state.

Bert Faylor, of Benkelman, Nebraska, attended a picnic on May 30, 1935, and complained to his neighbors as his family went home that evening, "It ain't a-gonna rain no more." Within twenty-four hours, he, his wife and two of his children, along with over one hundred others in the valley, had drowned, sucked by the Republican into a watery grave.

The flood forever changed the course of the river and its tributaries and altered the lives of those along its banks. It roared out of the night, spawned by a unique sequence of events. Stories of tragedy and heroism echoed down the valley as those in the path of the river fought to survive.

By the time the flood ended, those who had grown up on the Republican's banks no longer recognized the land they called home. Within hours, stories of the epic disaster, complete with tales of amazing heroism and unwavering courage, made their way into the history of the Republican Valley.

Chapter 1

THE RIVER—ITS GEOGRAPHY

The Republican drains an area of 22,400 square miles, or over 14.3 million acres. Jon Farrar described the river in the April 1995 issue of *Nebraskaland* magazine: "Winding serenely through nearly treeless grasslands, it offers no hint of where it has been, what it will become or what it once was." It stretches over 445 miles through three states. With headwaters in Colorado, it cuts through a small corner of northwest Kansas, enters Nebraska near Haigler and then travels through the southern part of the state to Superior. There, it moves back into Kansas, continuing on to Junction City. Tributaries in Colorado extend southwest over 100 miles to Limon. Northern tributaries extend as far north as the Platte River. The river is fed by many creeks and streams as far as 50 miles south in Kansas.

In the Republican Valley, the land rises and falls. The wind moves the grass, imitating waves on a tranquil green ocean. Stretching above this sea of grass, the vast dome of the heavens is visible to the horizon from almost every point on the compass. With a beauty all its own, the valley appears tinted with every color in nature's paint box.

These colors change with the seasons. From its springtime shades of green, the prairie ripens and turns to shades of gold in the heat of the sun. The rich earth warms, and rain refreshes the air. Winds move the prairie grass until the whole landscape seems to be undulating in the wind. Nature's canvas changes daily as grains and grasses mature in summer. In the fall, shades of brown, gold and red tint the hillsides and plains. In winter, frost

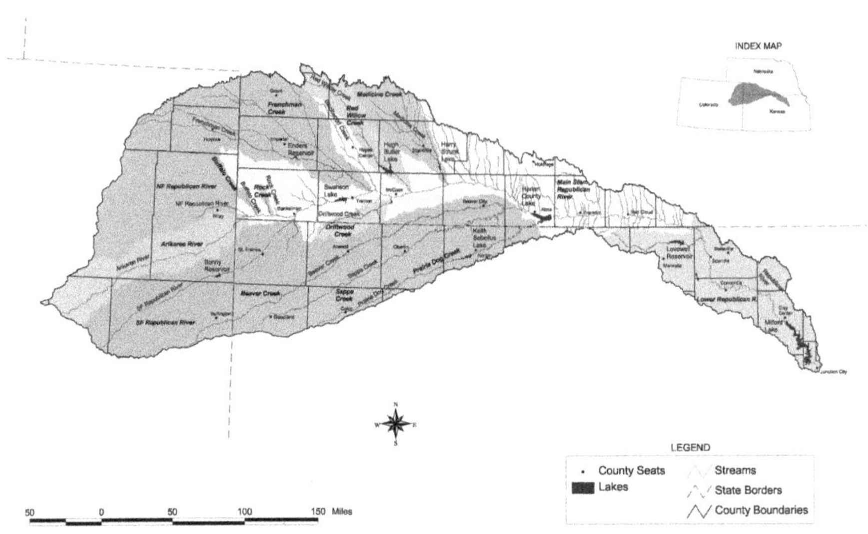

Map of the Republican River Basin. *National Weather Service.*

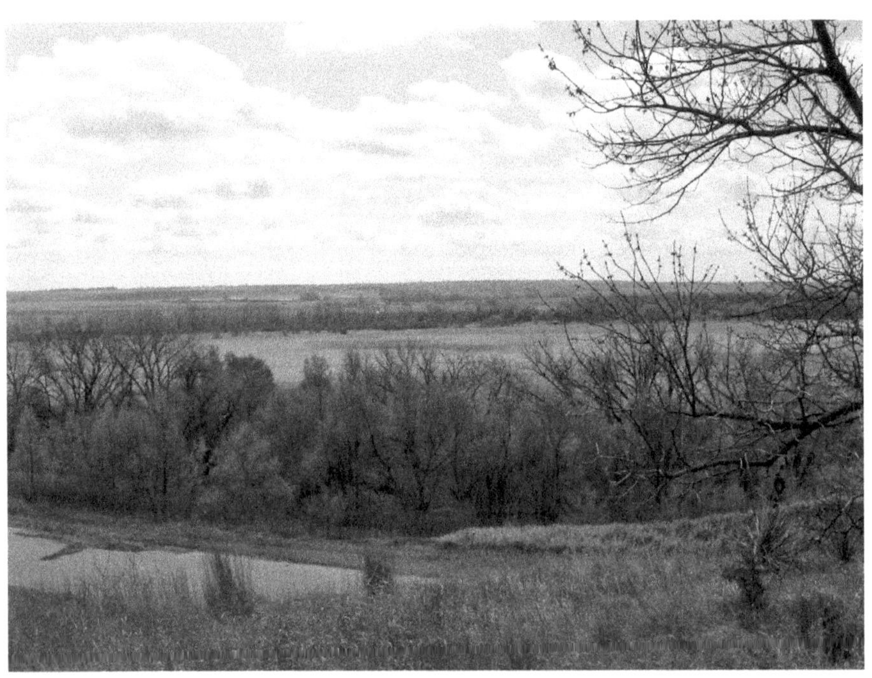

Photo of the bluffs of the Republican near McCook, Nebraska. *Author's collection.*

and snow make it difficult to tell where the horizon ends and the leaden sky begins over the cold and barren plains.

The sky changes as each day passes. Muted colors in the mornings give way to an expanse much like a watercolor painting with cirrus clouds tinted rose and gold. Sometimes the sky is cloudless, filled with infinite shades of cerulean blue. At night, far from the artificial lights of farmhouses and small towns, the crystal lights of countless stars crowd out the darkness. Some stars appear so close it seems possible to reach out and touch their icy light. On nights when the moon is full, it hides the starlight with its glimmering radiance.

The Republican flows through a wide river basin, bounded by steep bluffs once noted by John C. Fremont in his report about the area in 1842. A carpet of prairie grasses blankets the land. In the valley, buffalo grass is common, with yucca, sagebrush and some small cactus found in many areas. Trees are found in populated areas or near abundant water but do not flourish elsewhere due to the periods of prolonged drought. Those that do grow near water in the valley include cottonwood, hackberry, willow, some elm and ash. Bison, antelope and deer are native to the area and, before the 1860s, roamed the valley by the thousands. Small animals are still plentiful and include rabbits, raccoons, prairie dogs and skunks. A large variety of birds, bats and insects are also native to the area.

In his book *High Water Mark*, Raymond Borchers explains that the river is not named for a political party but for a local native tribe. The Pawnee occupied the area in the early 1800s. Labeled "Republican" because of their representative form of government, they lived in the area until about 1815, when they moved west, forced out by an increasing inflow of homesteaders. As part of the nation's Great Plains, the broad, shallow river valley is characterized by smooth grasslands. Today, farmers' fields bordering the river appear from the air to be random squares and circles in a giant green-and-brown patchwork quilt stitched together by miles and miles of wire fences.

A United States geographical survey conducted from Fort Riley, Kansas, in 1896 documented the twenty thousand acres in its military reservation and described the Republican River Valley as it appeared when the plains were first settled by homesteaders.

Multiple reports conducted by the United States Department of the Interior in the years following the initial Fort Riley survey characterize the soil in the majority of the Republican River Valley as loess top soil, often sandy and deposited by the shifting winds. Below this is a layer of alluvium sediment made up of non-stratified rock and sand. Annual precipitation in the upper valley is usually between sixteen and twenty-five inches. The

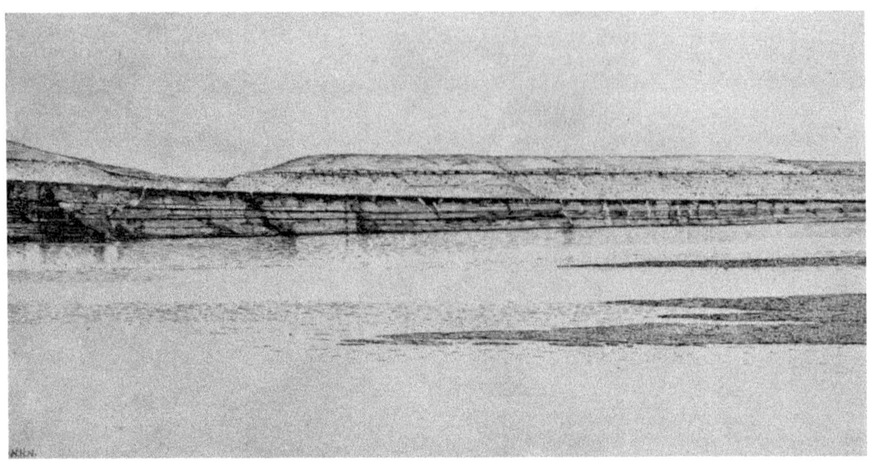

An 1896 drawing of the Republican River Valley. *USGS Bulletin No 137.*

climate in the valley includes warm summers and winters that are usually dry and cold. The land is scoured by almost consistent and abrasive wind and is crisscrossed by creeks with broad streambeds bordered by terrace-like bottomland rising to steep bluffs, some over 150 feet high.

The valley's elevation varies widely. At 5,365 feet at the river's headwaters in Colorado, it begins its descent, dropping an average of 10 feet per mile as it moves east. The river descends most dramatically between Haigler and Benkelman, Nebraska, dropping over 300 feet in about twenty-four miles. In this particular segment of the plains, the river has cut deeply into the valley, creating steep canyons with treacherous walls. Most of the tributaries joining the Republican are quite short, with a total stream fall of 200 to 300 feet, delivering water into the main channel very quickly. The river leaves Nebraska at an elevation of about 1,598 feet.

The junction of the North Fork of the Republican and the Arikaree River join near Haigler to create the main body of the Republican River. The South Fork of the Republican connects with this greater flow about 24 miles east at Benkelman. The river flows past many small towns in Nebraska to a location about 4 miles east of Superior, Nebraska, where it turns southeast into Kansas. It unites with the Smoky Hill River near Junction City, forming the Kansas (or Kaw) River in a course totaling well over 445 miles.

The average river channel measures about 150 feet in width with an average depth of 10 feet. In some places in the northwestern portion of the valley, the river dwindles to no more than a stream, which in the summertime is often less than 3 feet wide. The area on either side of the river where

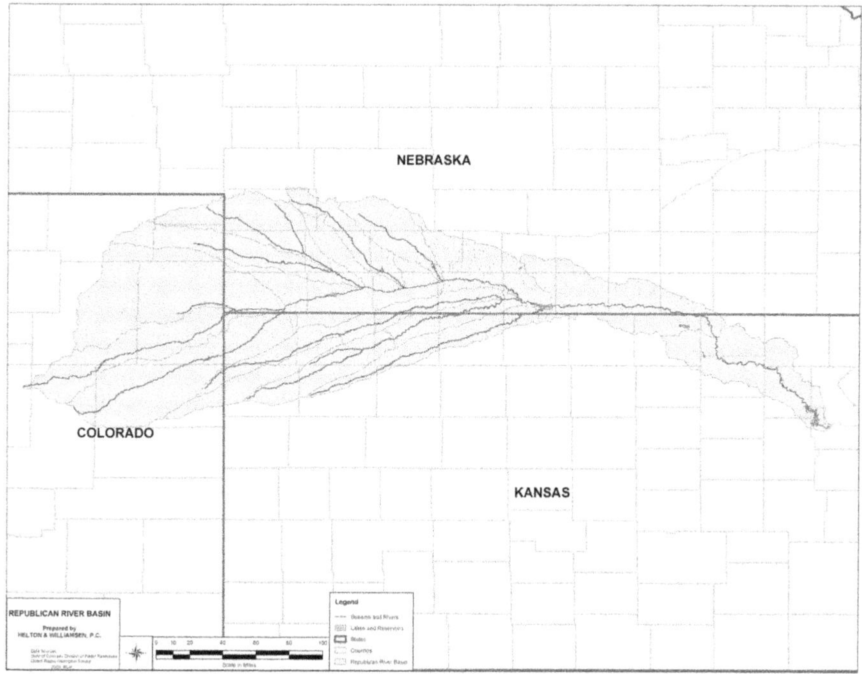

The Republican River Basin. *Republican River Water Conservation District.*

flooding most often occurs is locally termed the "first bottom," with the higher ground adjacent to this low land labeled the "second bottom." The width of the river and these bottomlands is about two miles in most places, with bluffs rising 150 feet to the surrounding "high plains."

Chapter 2

THE RIVER—ITS HISTORY

Native people made their home along the Republican for thousands of years. The remains of great buffalo hunts and the tools used by people from both the Clovis and Folsom periods can still be found near the river, according to Waldo Wedel, a former archaeologist at the U.S. National Museum in Washington, D.C. One such site, the Jones-Miller Bison Kill site on the Arickaree River near Laird, Colorado, in the Upper Republican Valley, reveals evidence of their environment ten thousand years ago. Much like today, the archaeological record catalogues drought, dust storms and the impact these changes made on the people living in the area.

Archaeologists found remnants of the Upper Republican culture in the valley in Nebraska and in northeast Colorado. These tribes lived in square earthen lodges and inhabited the area from AD 1000 to AD 1500. The Dismal River culture also entered the area, especially west of the 100th meridian.

According to Robert Blasing, in a report prepared for the National Park Service, many Central Plains tribes lived in the Republican River Valley in the fifteenth century. They survived on corn and fish. According to the report, anthropologists found the remains of a large Native American village in the Medicine Creek Valley of Nebraska. It is believed the inhabitants abandoned their homes about the time Coronado was marching through the area in 1541. Evidence suggests they were driven out by floods and droughts that destroyed their food sources.

In some locations, several inches of soil, deposited by the ceaseless wind, separate archaeological sites in the same location. These soil deposits indicate that the area was abandoned by one culture for many years before another completely different people repopulated the area.

Later, the Sioux, Cheyenne and Arapaho tribes crisscrossed the valley. Labeled the Plains Tribes by white settlers, they followed the great bison herds that roamed the area. These tribes had diverse languages and customs. All lived in large villages located near streams in order to be near water, wood and tillable land. According to Julene Bair, a local author who grew up near the Republican, the Cheyenne told pioneer settlers they called the area the "Ladder River Country" because they could travel from stream to stream along the main channel, always in reach of water on the plains.

The Pawnee made their homes along the Republican's banks in permanent agricultural villages, living in circular lodges partially submerged in the earth. White settlers expressed little interest in the Native American land during the early migration west because of its location, which was too far from either the Santa Fe or Oregon Trails. While the Pawnee retained possession of the valley, they constantly fought off attacks from the Cheyenne and Arapaho. Trappers and Native American traders visited the area but left no trace of their passage. Oral history and pictographs recorded on buffalo skins found among the native tribes told of floods in 1711, 1712, 1781, 1826 and 1849. Archaeological digs in the area support these primitive historical records.

The *Lincoln Journal* of June 6, 1835, ran a story about a legend of the Pawnee tribe. This story, told for hundreds of years among the Pawnee, explained what they knew about the Republican River.

The people left a beautiful garden and traveled west in search of buffalo. There, the medicine men learned to live with the wild animals, and the animals shared their wisdom. These men reported seeing giants in the area, a proud people who did not obey the gods. As a punishment for their pride, the gods sent a great rain. The race of giants laughed. Ignoring the rain, the giants waded defiantly into the river through the mud and slime. The rain continued, creating a great flood. The giants, trapped in the mud, drowned as the river rose higher. The medicine men explained to the people that the giants received a fitting punishment for their disobedience.

As the Pawnee people hunted for buffalo, their medicine men pointed to giant bones visible in the banks. They explained that these bones belonged to the race of giants. Exposed each spring along the shores of the river, the bones served as a reminder to the Pawnee not to be too proud or their gods would send a flood to kill them, too.

The United States acquired the valley as part of the Louisiana Purchase in 1803. Lewis and Clark mention the river in their report to Jefferson in 1804.

One of the first visits to the area by an American military expedition came under the leadership of Zebulon Pike in 1806. In 1842, John C. Fremont followed the river as he traveled to Colorado. At his camp on a fork of the Republican at a height of 2,350 feet, he named the Prairie Dog River, near Alma, Nebraska, for the creatures surrounding his camp. He described the Republican River at this location as being about 40 feet wide and twelve inches in depth, with banks lined with ash, maple, cottonwood and willow. Traveling west, past the 100th meridian, the land changed abruptly. As the elevation increased, the expedition discovered bare sand hills surrounding the river with the water running inches deep and about 600 feet in width in a shallow bed of yellow-white sand. The river ran through an almost treeless landscape, traveling among broken ridges or bluffs, some rising quite high on either side. Thousands of buffalo watered along and in the river.

According to the Bostwick Division report, created by the United States Bureau of Reclamation for the area encompassing the Republican River, after enactment of the Homestead Act of 1862, European immigrants became interested in the fertile Republican River Valley. Encouraged by a cycle of abundant moisture and the invention of barbed wire to protect their plowed fields, settlers surged into the valley.

European settlers shared their stories of great floods also. An immigrant reported that he witnessed a great flood in the valley in 1849. He told of seeing vast buffalo herds drowned and hanging in the tops of trees. A heavy frost preserved the dead animals until spring. With that thaw came a cholera outbreak, devastating to both the settlers and the Native American tribes in the area.

Residents reported a flood in 1869. Witnesses saw entire families of settlers swept away, with a few lonely survivors clinging to the tops of trees, hoping for rescue. One story told of a tiny baby wrapped in an adult's shirt tied high in a tree surrounded by rushing water. The child cried for hours before those on shore could secure a boat to attempt rescue.

Although Native Americans who remained in the valley warned of "big water" extending "bluff to bluff," residents ignored their advice, lured by the promise of free land and good river-bottom soil. Homesteaders who came to work the land, like the primitive cultures before them, tended to follow the river because of the easy availability of water and the timber necessary for shelter and firewood.

In addition to the rich farmland, many considered the valley a paradise for hunters. The legendary Doc Carver, one of the greatest marksmen in the country at the time, reported seeing at least 500,000 buffalo when he rode into the valley. His friend at the time, Buffalo Bill Cody, along with the support of Seventh Cavalry troops, organized a buffalo hunt for the Grand Duke Alexis, brother of the czar of Russia, northwest of McCook, Nebraska, in January 1872. Aided by the Sioux, the hunters enjoyed great success. The Duke marveled at the abundance of wildlife and the wide expanse of prairie land.

The Pawnee relinquished their rights to the river in a treaty signed in 1857 but retained hunting privileges along the Republican. This ended in 1873, when they were attacked by their traditional enemies, the Brule and Ogallala Sioux, in Massacre Canyon while on a hunting expedition near Trenton, Nebraska. By 1875, the Pawnee had been moved to a reservation in Oklahoma along the Arkansas River.

In 1874, a plague of grasshoppers stripped the fields of all the crops growing in the area. After eating all the wheat, oats and corn, the "hoppers" turned to the trees, stripping them bare. In 1875, a prairie fire swept through the valley, destroying everything in its path.

Undeterred by these events, those who stayed envisioned an irrigation system harnessing the power of the river, taming the land and increasing crop yields. These settlers established their farms and built churches and schools. With the coming of the railroads in 1880, towns sprang up all along the river. Highways followed the railroad tracks. At first, people crossed the river at their own risk, but soon strong bridges spanned the most-traveled routes. Crossing the river became easy for those traveling the valley.

Terrible blizzards in the winters of 1885–87 devastated the area, killing the local cattle industry. These years were followed by ten years of drought, which caused widespread crop failures in the valley. The economic depression of 1893 compounded the area's problems. Spring flooding and prairie fires further discouraged many would-be farmers, who gave up and moved.

The rain returned after the turn of the century, and more land went under the plow as agricultural product prices rose. Residents recorded spring flooding in 1885, 1903, 1905, 1915 and 1923. The economy took a downturn in the early 1920s, followed by a series of extremely dry years. The grasshoppers also returned to compound the misery of those trying to make a living along the Republican.

For the residents of the valley in the 1930s, the river wound through their fields and their lives like a honeysuckle vine winds through a fence. Soon the vine and the fence become inseparable, and cutting one damages the other. In just this way, the river became an integral part of the life of the people, and the people in turn took life from the river.

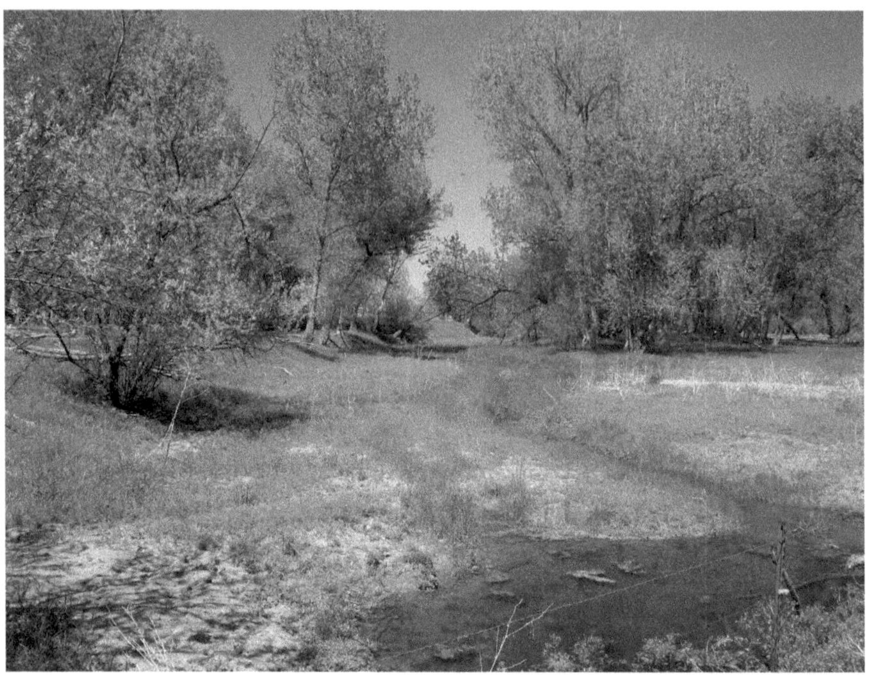

The quiet beginnings of the North Fork of the Republican River in Colorado. *Author's collection.*

During the spring, the river ran noisily through the valley as water raced to the east. In the summer, the river dried to a trickle, often running only ankle deep. Great sandbars appeared in the middle of the riverbed. The water ran clear, with a fine sand bottom. Children playing along the banks could easily see the minnows and other fish swimming in the lazy water.

The grassy banks became the perfect spot for a picnic or a friendly game of baseball when neighbors weary from a week of often-backbreaking work gathered after church. In the winter, the river disappeared, peacefully sleeping beneath a blanket of ice and snow. Ernest Purvis of Cambridge, Nebraska, remembered ice-skating to school across its smooth surface. Families cut ice along its shores to store for summer use.

Spring floodwaters ran icy cold and full of debris from nearby fields. The water cut into the banks until they towered twenty to twenty-five feet above the river. These unreliable banks gave way easily. The soil and rock collapsed under the weight of men or animals foolish enough to venture too close to the edge of these dangerous precipices.

In Marlene Wilmot's book *Bluff to Bluff*, Bessie Orcutt Keegan recounted that before the 1935 flood, a ninety-seven-year-old Native American returned to the valley to visit his tribal homeland and warned that her home on the Republican would be flooded. He warned her that the river would rise again. He told her, "Lady, you shouldn't live here; water will be bluff to bluff." Bessie, like everyone else in the area, did not heed his warnings. More and more people drew closer to the river to try to make a living on the rich bottomland of the Republican and its tributaries.

Chapter 3

THE DIRTY THIRTIES

Lee and Lottie Guthrie and their eight children, a farm family from Indianola, Nebraska, lived near the river during the 1930s. Similar farmsteads like theirs dotted the area, often with less than a half mile between each family home in rural areas. In Nebraska, according to the 1930 U.S. Census, more people lived in the Republican River Valley than at any time in history. Often, large, extended families and even hired workers all lived together in one household.

Many families settled in the Republican River Valley following the Homestead Act. As the valley revealed its cycles of abundant rainfall followed by years of drought, some abandoned their homesteads. Local history does not document the numbers who gave up and moved back east or farther west. Diaries and other accounts reveal that some of those who stayed were often either unable to afford the cost of moving or were too stubborn to give up.

Families who stayed were bound to the land by multiple bonds. They loved one another, and they loved the land. Farming and small-town living was a way of life. Staying together and owning their land or a business was often the dream that originally brought their family to the valley. Whether in town or in the country, hard work with few, if any, laborsaving devices kept most people busy every day. Some families worked especially hard, having a business in town and a small farm in the country.

On the farm, work started at daybreak and often lasted until darkness fell. Some families did their fieldwork with the help of tractors and the latest

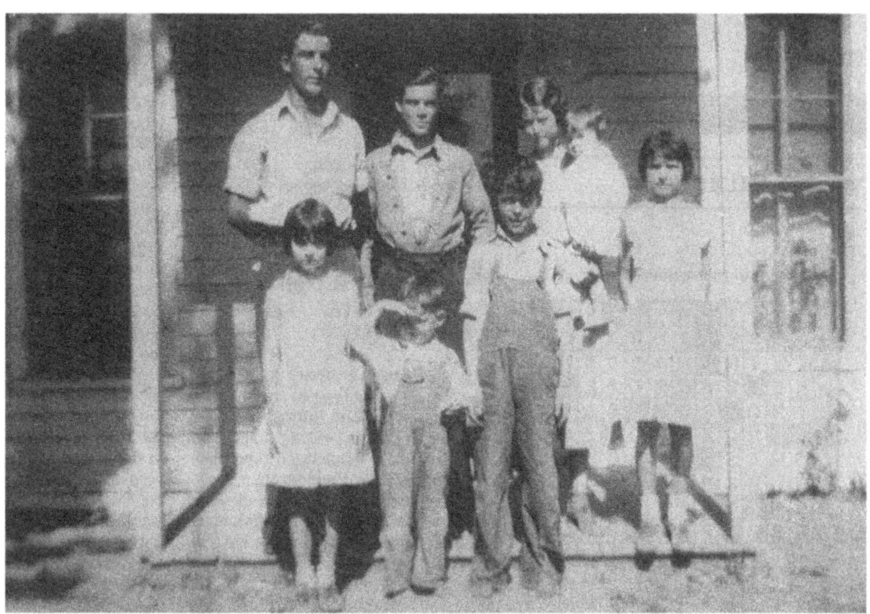

Children of Lee and Lottie Guthrie, Indianola, Nebraska. Pictured in the front row are Opal, Lewis, Lyle and Gail. In the back row are Carl, Dean and Leah, holding Ruth. *Author's collection.*

farm implements. Others relied on horses to prepare their fields and harvest their crops. Large threshing crews often consisted of a group of neighbors. They banded together and followed the harvest from farm to farm, sharing labor and equipment as crops ripened.

Many families raised livestock for food and for cash sale. Stock included beef and dairy cattle, hogs, sheep and poultry. Chickens and ducks provided eggs and meat. Cows provided cream and milk, as well as meat. Excess farm products, not needed for use at home, could be traded in town for flour, sugar, coffee, fabric for clothing and other necessities. Families planted large gardens that provided fresh vegetables in summer. They canned excess vegetables for winter, along with fresh potatoes and carrots, stored in cool dugouts or storm cellars.

Women and children worked on the farm and at many businesses. Household duties kept all family members constantly busy. Laundry, most often done with a washboard or a gas-powered wringer washer, took all day. Some rural homes piped water in the house from the river or a nearby well or stream. Many families carried water from the river or stream into the house, while some homes used a cistern that collected

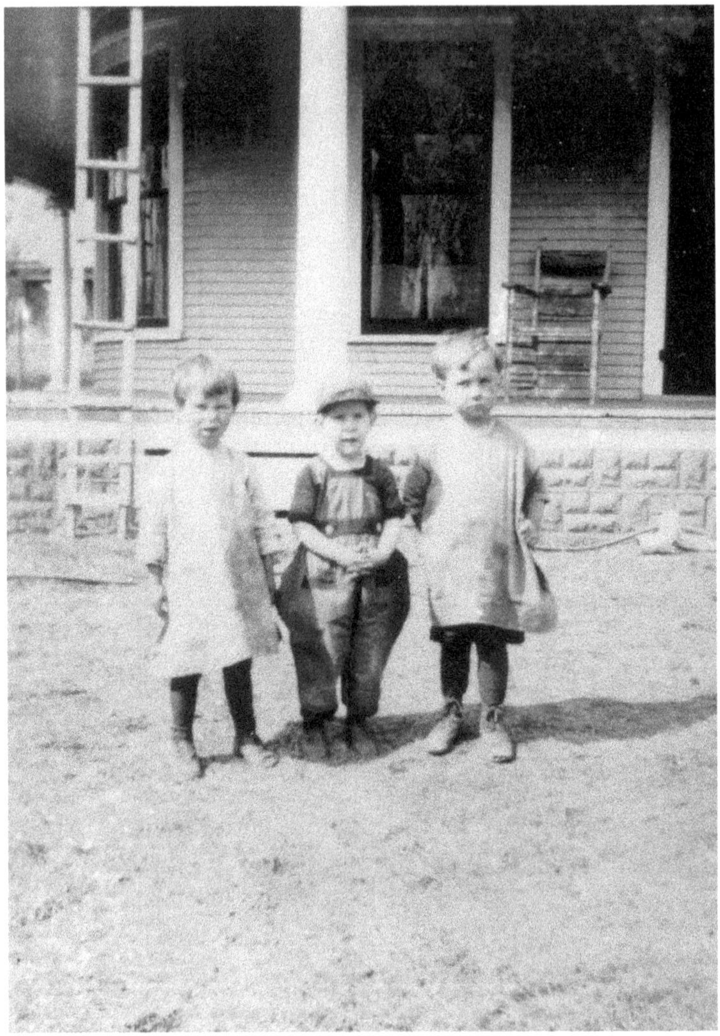

Children near Alma. *Joseph Torrey.*

rainwater for reuse inside the home. Few homes had special rooms for bathing, so families heated water on the cookstove and filled portable washtubs or bathtubs manually.

Most families relied on someone in the household to make their clothes. Careful mending lengthened the life of each garment. Large families passed clothing down from child to child. Most families did not have closets full of clothes for each family member. Often, children owned one outfit for "every day" and one other to wear to school or church. Children wore underwear made of cloth flour sacks. Many children took great pride in a store-bought dress or overalls.

Clothing passed from sibling to sibling until no longer fit for wear. Thrifty homemakers cut up and pieced the remaining useable fabric into quilts; if extremely worn, the garment took on a new life in the ragbag. The thrifty home's ragbag recycled old clothes into makeshift cleaning cloths. Many farmers also used these rags as material for bedding for sick animals brought into the house in the hope of nursing them back to health.

Homes, often simply built, stood on little or no foundation. Many homes did not have plumbing or electrical lines to tether them to the ground. Few, if any, homes in rural areas in the 1930s enjoyed the luxury of electricity. Most still relied on kerosene or oil lamps for lighting. Many heated their homes with the cookstove in the kitchen and a heating stove in the parlor. Fuel sources included wood or coal, although some families still used hay twists and prairie coal (dried animal dung) rather than more expensive sources of fuel.

Many families, both in town and on the farm, did not own a radio or telephone. They relied on neighbors or the mail for news. If a home did have a radio, it still might not operate because the home's location was too far from the radio station. Battery-powered radios suffered short battery life. To conserve power, homeowners used the radio at only select times of the day, often at noon, when the family gathered for the main meal of the day.

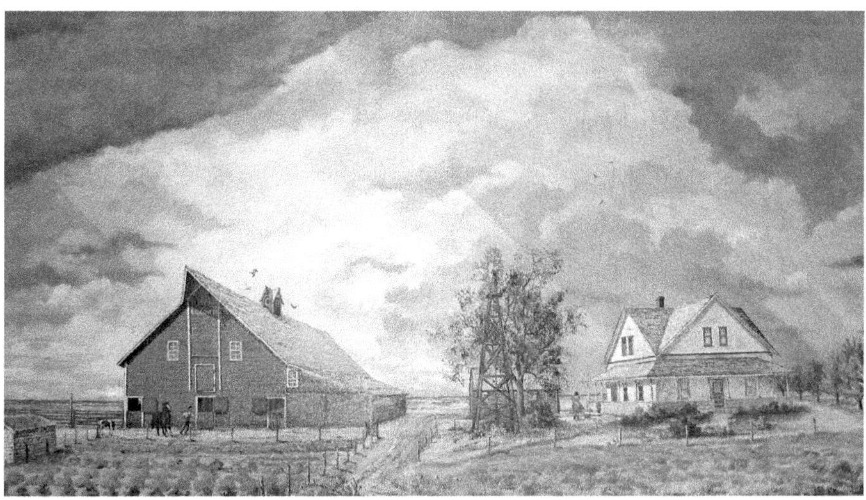

The Lester Confer home (typical of other farm homes in the area) before the flood. *Author's collection.*

Telephone lines strung along gravel roads in rural areas did not always hang on telephone poles but instead connected directly to the wire fences crisscrossing the country. The phones, large wooden boxes that hung on the wall in kitchens and parlors, used a crank-type ringer to contact a central operator. Few families could afford a private telephone line and instead shared a line with several neighbors. Sometimes six or more families shared a single telephone line. When a call was placed on these "party lines," the telephone rang into all the homes on the same line. The telephone company assigned each family their own distinctive ring so that residents could decide who should answer the call. Families knew when to answer by the type of ring they heard. A "general" ring meant that the call applied to everyone on the line.

Although many families owned cars and trucks, farmers still depended on draft animals such as horses and mules for transportation. Except for a few paved highways, rough dirt and gravel roads laced with deep ruts and holes, especially after heavy rain, crisscrossed the country leading to individual farm homes. A saddle horse or a team of horses and a wagon fared far better than a car or truck when traveling from place to place in rural areas.

Small communities thrived in the area. These towns gave farmers a place near their farms to sell crops and purchase supplies. Small-town businesses provided for most of the needs of the surrounding population. Each community had its own schools, churches and government offices. Most small towns had at least one church, a post office, a grocery store, a movie theater, a restaurant and, often, specialty stores for purchasing hardware or farm supplies that could not be acquired easily from mail-order catalogues.

In 1935, a dry goods store in Nebraska offered wool skirts for \$1.39, and a man's suit sold for \$9.95. Sirloin steak sold in a small grocery store for \$0.19 a pound and coffee for \$0.33 a pound. Fresh vegetables offered for sale included new potatoes, six pounds for \$0.25, and fresh pears for \$0.19 each. Often, the produce and fresh milk and cream offered in the stores came directly from the gardens and barns of the area farmers.

With no one else to rely on, the people living along the Republican Valley relied on one another to survive. Perhaps because life was so difficult during the Depression years and because everyone shared the same situation all along the river valley, neighbors and extended families did whatever they could to help one another. When someone fell ill, the neighbors came and worked their fields, did their chores and cooked their meals. If a neighbor needed help to complete fieldwork, butcher a hog or clean chickens, other neighbors stopped to help.

Marlene Wilmot wrote in her book *Bluff to Bluff* that in 1930, corn sold for $0.52 a bushel. By 1932, it had dropped to $0.12 a bushel as the Great Depression worsened. The next year, it brought $0.05 a bushel. In 1934, it rose to $0.75 a bushel as the economy improved. The price continued to rise to a high of $1.10. But this bounty came too late to benefit local farmers. The drought took the corn crop before the corn reached maturity. There wasn't any corn to sell.

The value of farmland dropped more than 50 percent across the United States, falling from $78.4 billion in 1920 to $36.2 billion in 1933. Farm output dropped just as much, from $13.8 billion in 1920 to $6.8 billion in 1933. Unemployment rose to over 25 percent nationally. Years of doing without and never getting ahead began to take their toll all along the Republican River.

If falling land prices and unemployment weren't enough to bear, the drought that plagued the plains states became more than some residents could stand. The year 1934 remains one of the driest on record in the Republican Valley. In most places, a total of only five inches of rain fell during the entire year. Farmers worked their land continuously in futile attempts to get a crop. Lack of ground cover caused the incessant drying wind to move the topsoil easily. Cattlemen moved their herds to the river valleys, where some pastures still held water and provided some feed for the starving stock. Years of drought and dust storms left the pastures near their own prairie homes unfit to support any more than the family dairy cow. Many struggled to provide feed for any animals at all. Cattle suffered from malnutrition. Maxine Cadwallader of Oxford, Nebraska, remembered her father's purebred Herefords not producing a single living calf in the spring of 1934. Her father, forced to sell the entire herd, bore with grim determination this devastating blow, nearly fatal to their farm operation.

Dust storms became common as less and less vegetation held the topsoil. Short rainstorms deposited little moisture that quickly evaporated, useless to man or animal. The *Trenton Register* in Trenton, Nebraska, reported on March 15, 1935, that dirt poured from the sky in all directions. At times, the dust, so thick it completely blocked out the sunlight, created the need for streetlights in midafternoon. Road crews halted work. Their equipment's windshields became so scoured by sand that it became impossible to see the road ahead. Arthur Chaplin, of the Nebraska Highway Department, recalled, "If the wind was blowing strongly from the northwest, you knew you were going to have to put on a new windshield because it was just like glazed glass after those windstorms." Tumbleweeds blew into the fences. Dirt collected between the weeds until entire fencerows disappeared.

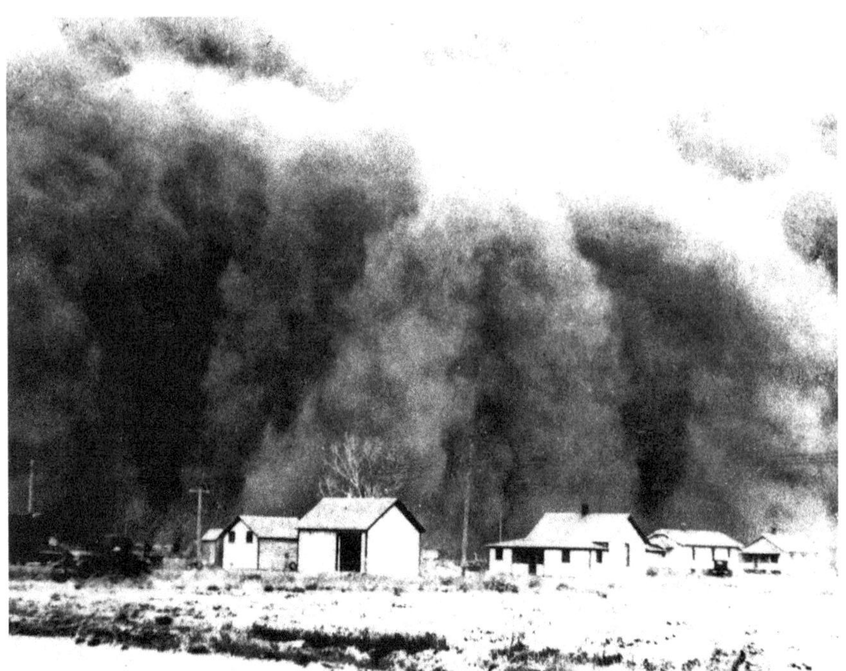

Nebraska dust storm. *Mary Sherk.*

If ill-fated travelers got caught on the road during a storm, they often drove off the road into the ditch due to poor visibility. When this happened, cars overturned and disappeared in wind-blown sediment. Often, these unfortunate folks and their vehicles vanished for years.

People who left their homes or businesses on errands or to travel often left the doors of their homes unlocked so that any passersby caught in these dust storms could take shelter if caught by surprise. This could be the difference between life and death, as the dust made it impossible to breathe and the scouring sand did permanent damage to eyes and lungs. The *Superior Express* reported on August 8, 1934, that to keep the temperature down and protect the newborn twin daughters of Mr. and Mrs. Will H. Gunn from the choking dust, blankets were hung around the outside of the Gunns' home and sprayed with water.

Chapter 4

The Rain Begins to Fall

In April, the *Republican Leader* in Trenton, Nebraska, reported a quarter inch of rain. The skies over the Republican Valley finally opened, and rain began to fall on the parched landscape. Hope turned to disappointment as more dust storms quickly followed these showers.

In early May 1935, as farmers admitted to themselves and their families that with no rain, they would no longer be able to stay in the harsh, unforgiving country, rains came like a blessing from heaven. At first, it seemed too good to be true. Mother Nature seemed to be showing her softer side, beguiling and bountiful, after years of unforgiving drought. Billowy clouds formed, and gentle rain fell.

May began with a trace of rain in the valley near McCook, Nebraska. Weather records reveal that it was quickly followed by a day with blowing dust. Then, a few more days of continued rain ushered in a pleasant spring. Farmers looked forward to getting into their fields in preparation for planting. Hopes rose in anticipation of a bumper crop, the first chance in many years. Several showers later in the month increased these hopes. The river rose briefly in the middle of the month but quickly dropped to normal levels. The saturated soil caused rain to run off, leaving water in all of the streams feeding into the river.

On May 30, 1935, Memorial Day, most commonly called Decoration Day at the time, the morning dawned pleasantly. In farms and villages along the banks of the Republican, children did their chores and played outside in the mild spring weather. Farmers checked the sky as they made plans for the

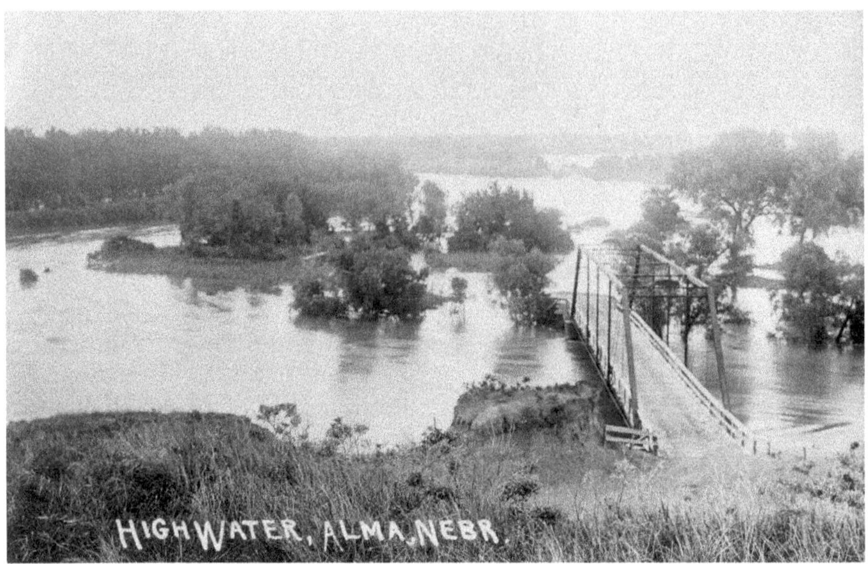

High water near Alma, Nebraska. *Joe Torrey.*

day's work. Many spent the day remembering those who gave their lives in service to their country. Others made plans to visit the graves of loved ones. These families cleared those graves of debris and placed flowers from their home gardens as tokens of remembrance for departed family, friends and honored dead. "Taps" echoed in the air, and rousing speeches honored those lost in the Great War in Europe, the Spanish-American War and the Civil War. People paused in their daily cycle of work to remember the past and to enjoy the day in the company of family and friends.

Few realized the severity of the storm clouds gathering on the horizon in the late afternoon. A major storm building over the headwaters of the Republican in Colorado came with little warning. Without the benefit of modern weather forecasting tools, the Weather Bureau, now known as the National Weather Service, created only daily weather maps. This information, provided to newspapers and radio, did not reach everyone in the Republican Valley. News, even about the weather, traveled slowly.

The maps for the period show an area of high pressure over the province of Alberta on May 28. According to Robert Follansbee and J.R. Spiegel, in a report to the U.S. Department of the Interior Geological Survey, this high-pressure system would gradually move over the Great Lakes in a clockwise flow, with barometric pressure topping out at 30.2 inches. At the same time,

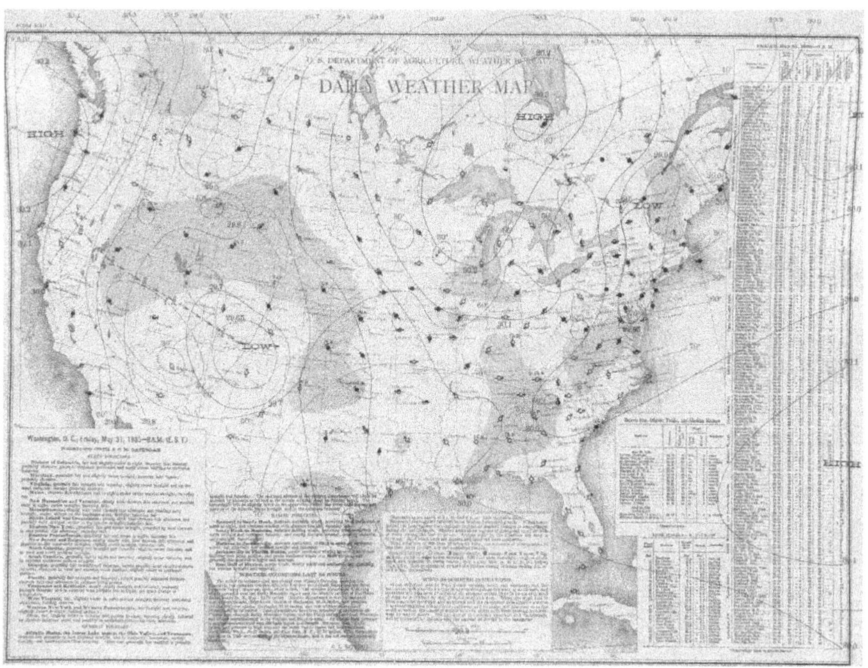

The May 31, 1935 Daily Weather Map. *National Weather Service.*

an area of low pressure moved through Arizona. By May 30, the system had moved over New Mexico with a pressure of 29.65 inches.

It soon advanced into southwestern Colorado, where its counterclockwise flow brought warm Gulf region moisture into the area. At the same time, the high-pressure area carried vast amounts of moisture from the Great Lakes. These two massive weather systems set the stage for the greatest flood in recorded history in the Republican River Valley. Within a few hours, on the boundary where the two systems collided on May 30, heavy precipitation began to fall.

The storm of May 30 through June 1, 1935, remains unique for many reasons, paramount the incredible amount of rain that fell. Where the Arikaree and Republican Rivers met in eastern Colorado, over twenty to twenty-four inches of rain fell in many areas in the short period of just a few hours. According to the *Seibert Settler* and government reports, a farmer in Newton, Colorado, owned a twenty-four-inch-deep stock tank that was dry before the storm. After the storm, it was running over from the heavy rain.

Reports of twenty-four inches in twenty-four hours came in from all along the South Fork of the Republican River, a record in the continental United

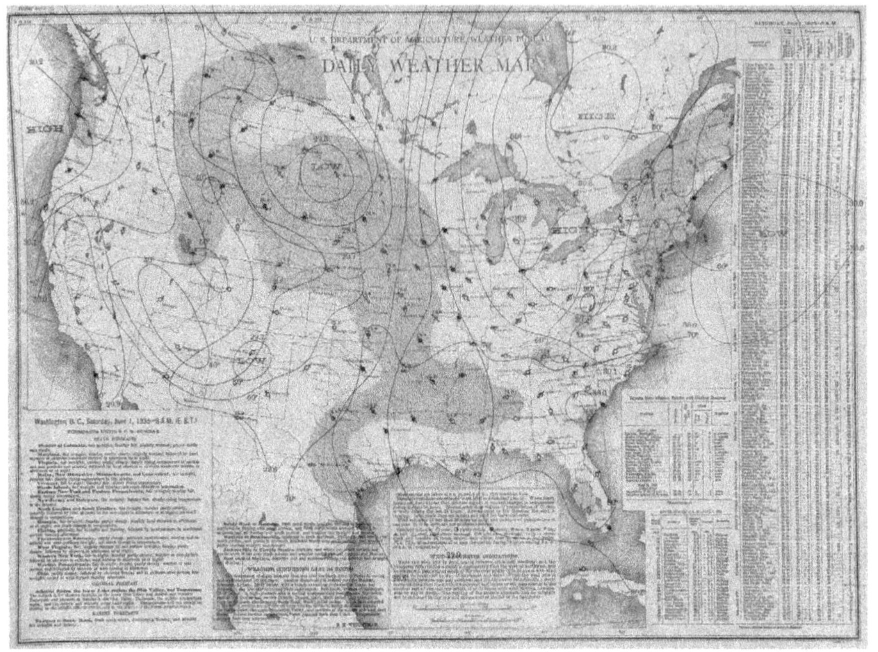

The June 1, 1935 Daily Weather Map. *National Weather Service.*

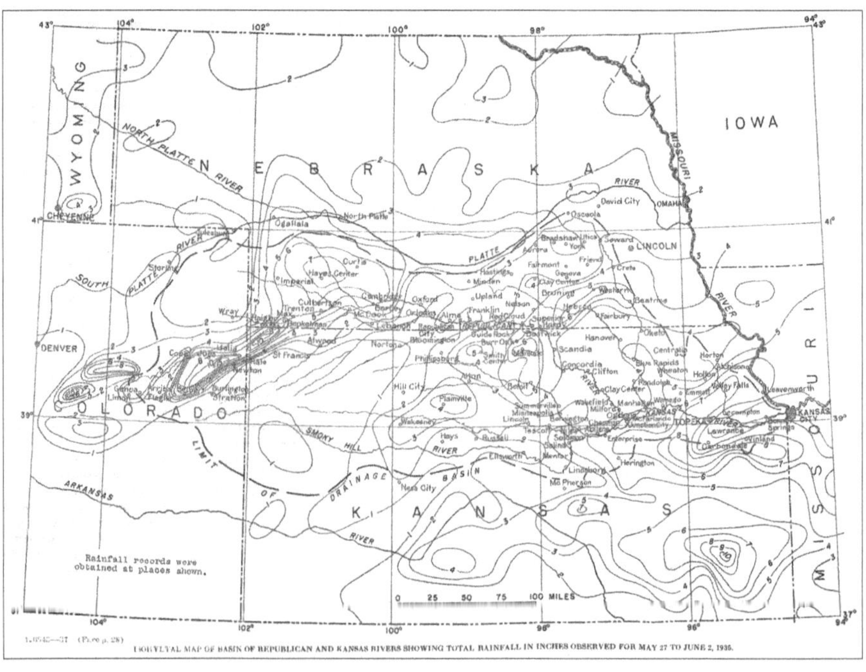

Rainfall totals from May 27 to June 2, 1935. *Follansbee and Spiegel.*

States at the time. The entire Upper Republican Valley received an average rainfall of nine inches. The severity of the storm increased because it did not stop raining. The storm continued to produce abundant rainfall as it followed the river's drainage basin from the headwaters of the Republican to Curtis, Nebraska, over 215 miles. As a result, the Frenchman, Red Willow, Medicine, Deer, Muddy, Turkey and other smaller creeks reached their flood peaks at the same time, just as the crest passed on the Republican River. An additional two to seven inches would fall in the basin before the storm ended.

When the two systems met over the headwaters of the Republican, many residents believed they were witnessing the end of the world. The suffocating downpour made the simple act of breathing extremely difficult. Incessant and vivid lightning accompanied by roaring thunder so loud normal conversation became impossible created a display of nature's fury unlike anything seen before. Mrs. Walter Joy lived twenty miles west of St. Francis, Kansas. She reported that the noise from the storm was so loud that the family had to shout to hear one another as they sat side by side watching floodwater creep under the door of their house. Although they were three-quarters of a mile from the river, it was not far enough away to avoid the approaching disaster.

According to the Nebraska State Historical Society, the flood began in the Republican Valley with a roar of water heard up to five miles away.

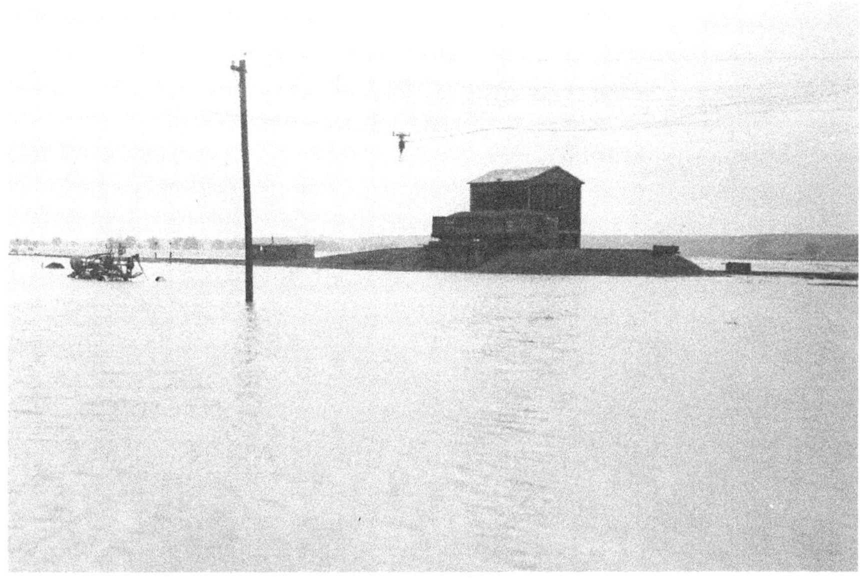

The river rises near St. Francis, Kansas. *Cheyenne County Museum.*

Many survivors reported two crests. Time and dates vary, according to the location of the residents along the river, but all agreed that the flood's second surge greatly exceeded the first. At one point, the water rose six feet in thirty minutes, ten to fifteen feet higher than any previous record crest. Eglantine Berger wrote her husband, telling him about the flood in Cambridge, Nebraska, one of the communities hardest hit by the flood. She wrote him that on May 31, 1935, the river began to rise. By 3:30 p.m., the northeast portion of the town, and much of the town south of the railroad tracks, was under water. The second crest hit town at 6:40 p.m., and she and her neighbors raced to the safety of a waiting truck, which sped to the top of a nearby hill.

Additional accounts printed in newspapers at the time state that the river rose 10 feet in twelve minutes in McCook. Nothing in the path of the wall of water survived unscathed. Water ran 20 feet deep in some places, with a discharge according to survey reports of an incredible 260,000 cubic feet per second—more than 320 times the normal flow today. Eyewitnesses reported water flowing "bluff-to-bluff," just as early Native American settlers had warned, even in areas where the bluffs stood at least two miles apart.

The river, in most areas flowing on open plains, rushed unconfined, making its own course down the valley. New channels sliced through the land, powered by the strong current as the water swiftly made its way regardless of what lay in its path. These new, more direct channels allowed the water to move at a rate faster than ever before.

Few, if any, had prepared for the terrible storm that scoured the High Plains in late May and early June 1935. Residents who already lived on next to nothing found themselves homeless. The river roared through the valley, carrying with it the wealth and the dreams of those who lived along its banks. It seemed as if all the rain the country had needed so much came in just a few hours, released all at once. Rumors spread of a great dam bursting somewhere in Colorado. Inaccurate newspaper accounts added to the misinformation.

Because deaths occurred in three states with little coordination or communication between local, state and federal government agencies, it is difficult to determine the exact number of people who lost their lives in the flood. Several attempts to create an accurate estimate list 110 to 113 killed—most reports just say "over one-hundred" dead.

The Department of the Interior's report of the epic flood lists a total of 830 miles of highway and 515 bridges destroyed, with over 274,000 acres of farmland submerged by floodwaters. In Kansas alone, over 1,400 homes were flooded. Damage estimates are almost certainly low—personal losses, bridges and agricultural and railroad losses are still almost incalculable.

Over twenty thousand head of livestock died in the high water. One report stated that carcasses littered the roads, making them impassable. Often impossible for their owners to identify, animals that survived their struggle with the furious river disappeared even if they made it through. Some animals, found as many as forty to fifty miles from home, blended in with the livestock of other families. Farmers who recovered such stock had no way of locating the rightful owners of stray animals.

Because of the ferocity of the storm and the lack of Weather Bureau precipitation stations, observers determined the amount of rainfall from improvised rain gauges. A "bucket survey," undertaken by Robert Follansbee and J.B. Spiegel, employees of the Department of the Interior, reported rainfall amounts from makeshift gauges such as cans, oil barrels and stock tanks made of metal and cement, the only gauges left standing after the storm passed.

Most towns in eastern Colorado avoided the direct path of the storm, but homes in rural areas experienced severe damage. The river began taking lives almost as soon as the flooding began. St. Francis, Kansas, lay in the direct path of destruction as the flood roared into that community at midnight.

The town of Haigler, Nebraska, survived because it is situated on higher ground. Other places in Nebraska, like Benkelman, Max, Stratton, Trenton,

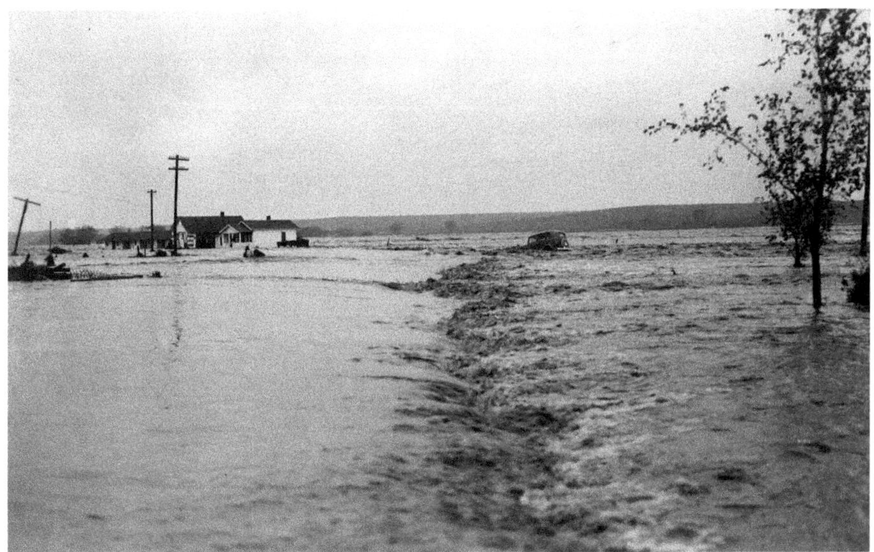

A car being washed away near St. Francis, Kansas. *Cheyenne County Museum.*

Culbertson, McCook, Indianola and Cambridge, suffered the river's wrath with great loss of life and property.

In some locations, farmers and townspeople had previously constructed earthen dams to build a reserve of water from the river and its tributaries. These earthen dams, located in Parks, Max, Maywood and Curtis, collapsed during the great flood, adding to the destruction both locally and downriver.

The river destroyed almost the entire hamlet of Parks, with one life lost there. In addition to the devastation, deaths also took place in Perry, Arapahoe, Orleans, Oxford, Franklin and Alma. Then the flood raged back into Kansas. Destruction and death followed in Concordia, Clyde and other towns along the Republican.

Some victims, last seen screaming for assistance from the tops of their homes, were swept downriver to certain death. Many watched helplessly as their entire lives changed in minutes. They were powerless to stop the persistent strength of the angry waters.

The death toll would have been much greater if people along the river had not risked their lives to help their neighbors. With no thought for themselves, heroes appeared in every community. Most were never recognized for their selfless acts of sacrifice. Some risked everything for flood victims they did not even know.

Chapter 5

The Flood Begins in Colorado

On the afternoon of May 30, 1935, Memorial Day, those who went to decorate graves and attend holiday events in eastern Colorado on the banks of the Arikaree, a tributary of the Republican River, enjoyed a pleasant afternoon. Many noticed dark clouds brewing on the horizon when they went to bed in the early evening. During the night, phenomenal amounts of rain fell. Residents in Colorado reported almost continual lightning with thunder that seemed to shake the ground, drowning out any attempts at conversation. Some went to bed with hopes for enough rain to sustain their crops, only to wake to find their fields scoured clean of both crops and topsoil.

The editor of the Stratton, Colorado newspaper, the *Stratton Press*, placed an ad meant to be funny in the paper days before the flood. It read: "Wanted: Rain." He later stated that seventeen inches fell in Stratton during the time of the flood. He speculated that it served as a reprimand for his attempt at humor.

V.S. Fitzpatrick, editor of the *Seibert Settler*, the Seibert, Colorado–area newspaper, reported on the storm in his book *Back Trail Disaster*. He and other residents watched the clouds on the horizon for much of the day on May 30. An inch of rain had fallen the week before, followed by hot sun and fifty-mile-per-hour winds, so no one worried about flooding from the approaching storm.

Toward evening, the rain began coming down in unremitting sheets of water with continuous thunder and lightning. The storm finally eased just after midnight, and Fitzpatrick slept peacefully. When he awoke the next

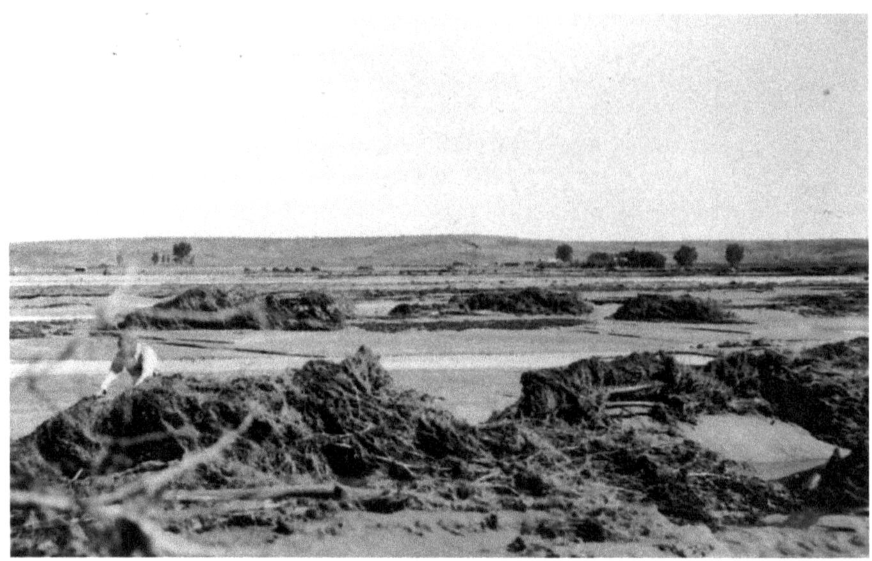

Searching for survivors. *Cheyenne County Museum.*

day, the town appeared to be swept clean. During the night, the driving rain's icy fingers had polished the store windows to a gleaming shine. All traces of the sand blown into every crevice by previous dirt storms vanished with the storm's scouring barrage. The town's population seemed to have also vanished, with stores left locked up tight and no one in sight.

Finally, Fitzpatrick found a workman at the hotel, who told him that the river had flooded in the night, cresting at about midnight. Neighbors and townspeople roamed the country, looking for survivors. Fitzpatrick dashed to the telephone to call the story in to the Associated Press but discovered that he could not even make a local call. He hurried to the railroad depot to send a telegram, only to find the telegraph lines out. In addition, tracks were out, and no trains would be coming from either east or west. The storm left Seibert completely cut off from the rest of the world.

Fitzpatrick later reported that brave rescuers, out at dawn, found a black swath of death and destruction where the river still roared. Houses in the lower valleys lay torn from their foundations. When the highway bridge between Seibert and Flagler collapsed under the pressure of the flood, it lodged against the railroad bridge. The debris in the floodwater collected against this unintended dam and created a lake of water behind the bridge. This put incredible stress on the railroad bridge, causing it to collapse. A surge of water cascaded into the already violent flood, causing even more destruction.

Survivors who escaped told of a night of terror. The Arikaree, which flows into the Republican, rose with two distinct flood crests several hours apart. The second crest, larger than the first, came during the darkest hours before dawn. The welcome morning light revealed new dangers as those marooned in trees and on rooftops realized they now perched in still-raging water surrounded by all kinds of animals both living and dead.

Adding to their problems, deadly snakes swam in the water, washed out of their nests along the riverbanks. Another danger, quicksand, filled the holes dug by the water, especially along the banks of the river, making rescue difficult or impossible. The water contained all sorts of debris—furniture, barrels, bottles, telephone and fence wire, clothing and even light bulbs could be seen rushing down the river. Thousands of dead jackrabbits, opossum, skunks, coyote, deer and birds polluted the water. The rich topsoil, formed over many millennia, vanished in the night. In many areas, the river left huge deposits of sand from a few inches to over two feet in depth, covering both the little remaining topsoil and the new crops already planted in the fields.

Six days later, Fitzpatrick reported the damage in his area to the outside world. He reported not only loss of life and property but also changes in the very ground around the small community. At first, he thought the volume of rain, over eleven inches at Seibert, had caused huge cracks to open in the ground, some over fifty feet in depth. Some of these cracks extended for miles and measured as much as six feet across. Below the surface, the roar of rushing water could be heard even days later. But the more he investigated, the more Fitzpatrick felt that the cracks must have been the result of an earthquake that occurred during the height of the storm.

Because Seibert found itself cut off from the outside world, Fitzpatrick could not notify authorities immediately. By the time workers had restored communications, the world no longer cared about what happened in the tiny community on the High Plains of Colorado, and geologists never surveyed the area. Meanwhile, nearby farmers, like the Hellings near Idalia, stood amazed when their lagoon, full of water after the flood, suddenly drained, revealing cracks stretching for miles to the horizon. As in so many other areas, water could be heard running in the depths below. The Hellings, like their neighbors, found no explanation. Life moved on, and work still needed to be done on the farm. Ever practical, they, like their neighbors, put fences up to keep livestock from falling in the crevices.

Nevertheless, Fitzpatrick mapped the location of the cracks with his own hand-drawn "earthquake" map. He wrote in his book, *Back Trail Disaster*, that he believed an escarpment lying between Genoa and Stratton,

Colorado, had slipped due to the electrical and magnetic tension created by the violent storm. He speculated that the violence of the storm had caused the movement, creating the cracks in such a wide area. Many of the local residents in the area still believe this to be true. However, James A. Dewey, of the United States Geological Survey, reported the following in June 2012:

> [Fitzpatrick's] *observations strike me as most consistent with the crack being the result of erosion by flood water—the report of gurgling water at depth within the crack seems to me to be a particularly strong indication of erosion by flood water, with the temporary stream that caused the erosion still carrying water from the saturated ground. Another possibility would be some kind of shallow failure of the ground, some kind of lateral earth flow, caused by the saturation of the soil, although I wouldn't necessarily expect gurgling water in such a situation. In the second case, one would expect to see that the crack occurred in an area with slopes, at the top of a slope.*

While the cracks in the earth might always remain a mystery and be the subject of much speculation, it might be important to note that one flood survivor reported that rushing water could still be heard coming from the cracks in the early 1950s.

Fitzpatrick noticed the flood also exposed mammoth bones buried in the riverbed. The flood scoured the plains so completely that the sites of multiple Native American villages were also exposed for the first time in hundreds of years. Additionally, countless buffalo skulls were revealed by the raging waters. In some areas, the river exposed giant tree trunks, indicating that, at one time, the river was bordered by a large, dense forest.

The first victims of the flood, Wayne and Frankie Gesner and Frankie's stepfather, Clarence Lothian, lived one mile west of Seibert, Colorado, along Sandy Creek. Their home stood over six feet above any previous high-water mark. A total of twelve inches of rain had fallen in their location during the storm, and their home lay in the direct path of the ever-widening river. When the fill from the railroad track gave way, it is estimated that their house, no match for the river's fury, exploded when hit by floodwaters over fifteen feet in depth at about 10:00 p.m. on May 30. Neighbors recovered Wayne's body about thirty-five miles from his home on the Corliss Ranch on June 2, 1935. It would be a few weeks before a landowner found Clarence's body near St. Francis, Kansas. Many weeks passed before Frankie's remains returned to be laid to rest.

The Rosser Davis family lived a few miles downriver from the Lothian place. They went to the upper floor of their home. Rosser got on the roof of the house and started waving a lantern, thinking he would warn his neighbors of the danger coming their way. But the waves swelled so high, and the rain fell so profusely, that no one could see his light.

The Davises' lost stock included a purebred draft mare. She became tangled in tree branches during the flood and drowned, finally coming to rest in the branch of a tree suspended ten feet above dry ground.

Days before the flood, Rosser had counted one hundred tall, old cottonwoods south of his house. After the flood, not a single tree stood on his place. Marvin Schaal visited the Davis home a few days after the flood. He reported that the waterline, evidence of the height of the water, went all around the room at the exact height of the keys on the family's piano. Every tabletop in the Davis house stood covered in mud. The family moved shortly after the flood. Rosser told friends that his mother had carefully chosen the site for the family homestead, wanting it to be close to water. After the flood, Rosser's wife refused to ever return to a home so close to the river.

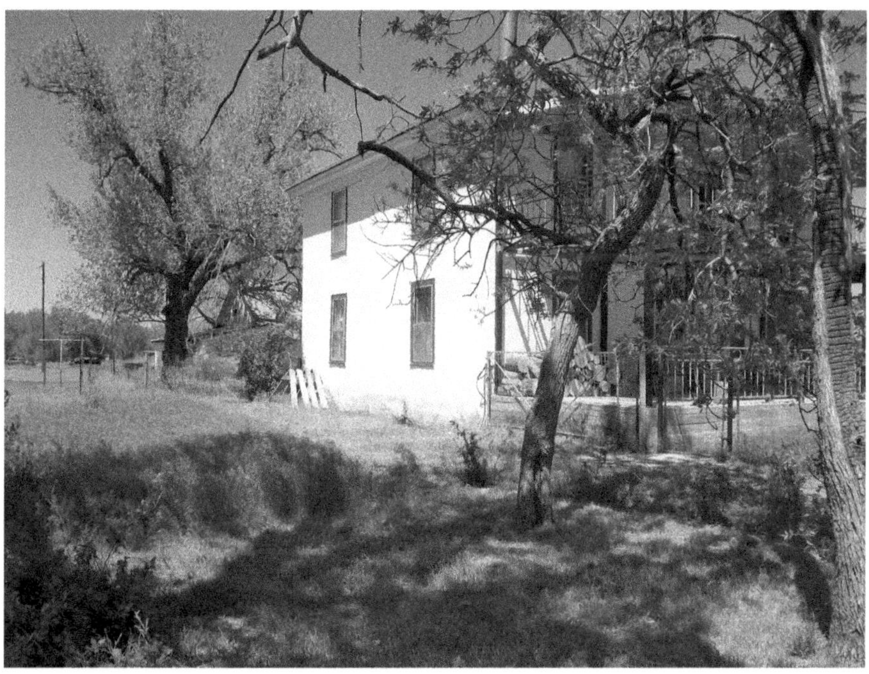

The Corliss home survived the flood. *Author's collection.*

That same day, May 30, 1935, Sherman Corliss and his wife, Grace, expecting another baby in August, worked at home along with their children: Betty, Lowell, Lyle, Mervin, Albert and Doris. Sherman's father, Albert, also lived with the family. Their farm, a pretty little place at the headwaters of the Republican, stood just east of several small lakes. Called the Corliss lakes by their neighbors, friends often gathered there with the family to enjoy good times together, including picnics, swimming and fishing. The land provided a good life for the Corliss family. Sherman built a strong house, two stories in height and made of concrete mixed on site.

On the day of the flood, the wind blew hard from the south. It started raining a little after dark. Hell Creek, Spring Creek and the South Fork of the Republican all came together about three miles from the Corliss home before joining with the Republican River, which ran along the south and east side of their property, about a half mile from the house. About midnight, the water splashed on the west side of their two-story cement house. The family began moving things upstairs, including flour, water, sugar and other perishable food. Fortunately, the floodwater never got into the house. At the peak of the flood, it lapped against the bottoms of the first-story windows.

Before daylight, the river roared over one mile wide through the valley, with the Corliss house in its center. Shortly after dawn on May 31, the water finally receded from around the home. The river remained high, however, making it unsafe to go out. The family stayed inside, secure in the cement house, trapped until the next day.

The river had dug out huge cottonwood trees near their home and, with fickle abandon, left its former course in search of a new, wider riverbed. Where the river once ran peacefully south of the house lay an abandoned sand-filled riverbed. The morning light illuminated the river, running swiftly east in a new channel a half mile north of the cement home.

The family lost thirty-three head of cattle and many hogs and chickens, a devastating loss for the family, as they depended on these animals to survive. Cows aborted their calves. Quicksand lurked everywhere. The Corliss boys spent hours rescuing animals from a sandy death.

The most distressing loss, four of their six horses, delivered a devastating blow to Sherman. It took six horses to pull a corn planter and four horses to pull a two-bottom plow. Their two surviving horses could not do the work needed for him to continue farming, and after the flood, no one had horses to sell. Compounding the problem, the river's rampage had slashed his fields, digging deep channels, some over one hundred feet wide and ten to fourteen feet deep, making fieldwork next to impossible.

Weeks after the flood, local boys sold cottonwood seedlings, which were sprouting all along the riverbanks. They bundled the trees together with sacking around the roots and then sold them twelve for a dollar to residents in nearby small towns. They also cut up the fallen trees ripped up by the roots during the flood. These trees provided a supply of firewood they could sell for cash.

As soon as Sherman could get out in a team and wagon, he took bedding, food and cooking utensils and moved to a rock house on higher ground, two miles southeast of their home. The family lived there through the summer of 1935, getting back to the cement house just in time for the children to walk to school on the sandbar south of the house.

It took a long time to get the ranch back in shape after the flood. Not a fence stood across the bottomland, and fences needed to be put up on the west and east as soon as possible so that surviving cattle would stay at the farm.

The Corliss lakes vanished, filled in with sand, the water replaced with weeds and cottonwood trees. Ancient tree trunks lay exposed along the channels cut by the flood near their home. The family also found freshly exposed Native American campgrounds, where the children discovered buffalo skulls, pottery, beads and arrowheads.

The loss of the Beecher Island Monument in Colorado dramatically illustrated the power of the flood. The large monument stood on an island commemorating a battle between soldiers dispatched from Fort Wallace, Kansas, and Cheyenne warriors, including Roman Nose, who fought along the Arikaree. In addition to this and other smaller monuments erected over the graves of the fallen soldiers on the island, the area included a campground and park. Carved from Silver Plume and light Barre granite, the large monument stood over eighteen feet in height from base to peak. The foundation rested on a twelve- by twelve-foot base sunk six feet into the ground. Forty-nine pilings, each eight feet long, installed in the bottom of the excavation touched bedrock, with the hole filled with broken stones, sand and cement. After the flood, the entire island disappeared, and the river changed channel. The white granite pylon disappeared with the island; the base remained tilted on end. Funds raised later replaced the old mighty monument with a smaller pylon. It is speculated that the rampaging river dug a huge hole near the site of the old monument, deposited the pylon in its watery grave and covered it with sand and silt.

The Arikaree in Colorado went from dry and barren to a raging torrent, over a mile wide in many places, within two hours. Idalia remained an island for several days after twelve inches of rain cut the community off from the

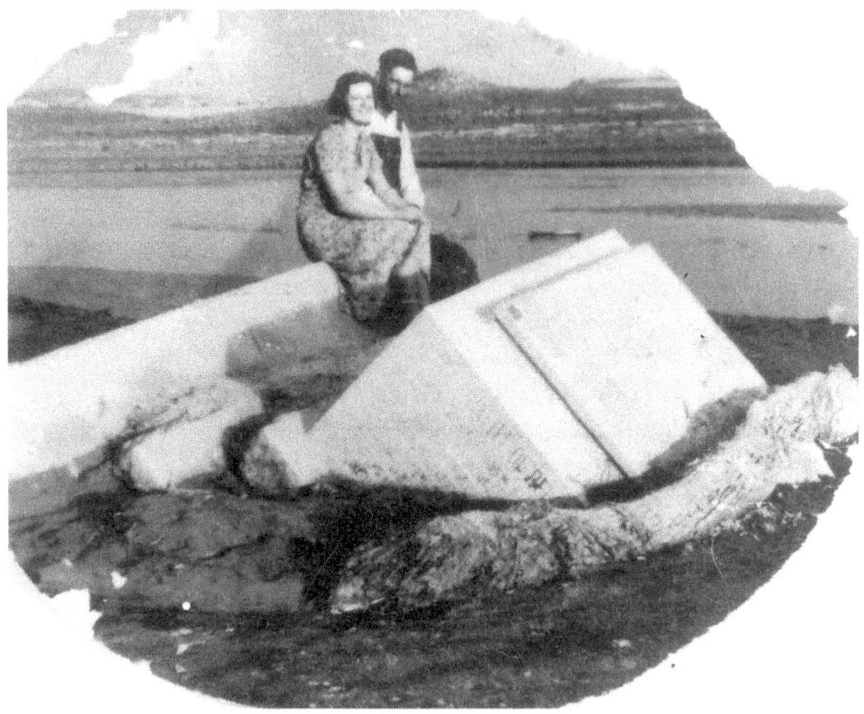

Jessie Wagner and Ward Wilson (who would later marry) on the base of the Beecher Island Monument after the flood. *Author's collection.*

surrounding area. Residents on the south side of the river stood watching, completely cut off from friends and family on the north side.

The river remained over a mile wide in the area for many days. The water raced on through Colorado. Bridges and roads disappeared, swept away as the flood consumed everything in its path. Debris and desolation lay in the river's wake. Those who went to watch the water race heard loud reports, sounding like rifle shots, followed by the collapse of a cottonwood tree, snapped at the roots. The tree then rolled down the river like a tumbleweed caught in a strong breeze.

Josiah "Si" and Harriet "Hattie" Harding raised ten children, but only four were at home on the night of the flood. Born in Ohio, Si and Hattie had married in Hebron, Nebraska, and moved several times before finally making their home on the Republican River near Hale, Colorado. The children at home that night included Myrtle, age nineteen; twins Alta and Alfred, fifteen; and the youngest, Rodney, age thirteen. They lived in a small house belonging to Si's employer, Ernest Wiley, who allowed the family to live there until they could save enough money to move to Si's brother's farm in Missouri. The house consisted of two larger rooms on the main floor, a kitchen and living room and a small bedroom for Si and Hattie in the back. It boasted a fine attic with a small window, and Si built a stairway so it could be used for the girls' bedroom. The boys slept in the living room.

Ernest paid Si a dollar a day to work for him, top wages for a farmhand in those days. Despite his good job, Si dreamed of moving to Missouri, where his brother Lloyd offered him sixty acres just for clearing the property. Si drew up plans to build a cabin from logs cleared from the Missouri place. To finance the house and the move to Missouri, he planted a garden of potatoes and onions on the river bottom near their Hale home. A merchant in St. Francis, Kansas, promised to buy all the vegetables the family could raise. The Harding family prayed for rain for their garden, hoping the fall crop would bring in enough extra money to finance their Missouri dream. The potatoes and onions came up but struggled to survive.

On May 30, 1935, the family spent the day working at home. The girls helped their mother sort beans for a supper of bacon and beans. Hattie baked bread. Alfred and Rod went along the river bottom to collect firewood where the river curved in a U shape before moving in to Kansas. Alta went along, and the children all enjoyed the green grass and the wildflowers blooming in the river bend. Rod, recovering from a recent illness, commented that a flood could sweep right over where they stood if it rained enough. They all laughed at the thought because none of the children could remember a time when the water ran in much more than a trickle. In fact, when it did rain, they would go and sit on the river bridge just to watch the water flow. Even the adults in their family could not remember a rain heavy enough to make the river leave its banks. They all knew the story about the Native American who warned people not to build in the Republican Valley, but no one they knew really believed the story.

When Alta and the boys got back from the river, they noticed clouds building in the west. Si came in from hoeing the garden and told them he expected they would be getting a rain that night. He instructed Albert to set a pan out in the yard where it could not be blown over by the wind so that they could measure the rainfall. In a wagon pulled by their team of horses, he and the boys returned to the river bottom to load the firewood the children had stacked there.

The girls helped their mother prepare supper. As the family sat down to a meal of fresh baked bread with Hattie's homemade jelly, beans with bacon and fried potatoes, it seemed almost like a celebration of the rain to come.

Hattie seemed pleased. The rain would water the flowers she had planted. Her sister, Mary Hudson, planned to visit, and Hattie kept the family busy with preparations. Hattie even made two new dresses for herself, something she rarely did, as the children always needed new clothing and she always put their needs first.

The family did not own a radio or have a telephone. Their news came from the paper, *Capper's Weekly*, which they received in the mail. Hattie would read the paper aloud to the family by the light of an oil lamp, due to the lack of electricity in their home.

On the evening of May 30, the family went to bed about 8:00 p.m. as the rain began and darkness came early. Lightning began to light the sky. The deafening thunder caused Si to comment that it sounded good to him. He told the children he would have a good night's sleep with the rain pounding on the roof. After such a hard day's work, they all slept well. The girls went to sleep almost immediately, as the rain on the roof hammered so loudly that they could not hear each other to talk.

Hattie awakened a few hours later when she felt something moving on her chest. She touched her breast and discovered a snake coiled on her chest. She screamed, and Si woke and reacted quickly, grabbing the snake and throwing it across the room. That is when he saw water pouring in through their bedroom window.

Si woke the boys and then went upstairs to wake the girls. He told all the children to get up and dress warmly, as the rising river might endanger the house. The family needed to move to higher ground, as water had already risen as high as the bedsprings in the downstairs bedroom. He urged them to stay with their mother while he went for the horses in the corral so they could all leave together in the wagon.

The girls dressed quickly, including putting on their winter coats, and joined their mother downstairs. Hattie wore three dresses—her two new dresses and her everyday dress—a securely buttoned winter coat and tightly laced shoes. She also took the time to wrap her very long hair in a tight bun. The girls saw their father standing at the front door. As he opened it, even more water came in the house. When the lightning flashed, the family saw the empty corral. The river had already taken the horses and left them with no way to reach safety.

Si began to calmly talk about plans for the family's escape. Only half of the assembled family could swim; Hattie, Alta and Rod had never learned. Si first told them he would take the family one by one to high ground. But he changed his mind after he broke out the window facing the hills. As the lightning flashed, he saw the water moving much too swiftly for the family to escape by that route. He suggested they move the kitchen table to the far corner of the room. They all stacked their things on the table to keep them dry, including quilts from their beds, and climbed up out of the water.

The family sat with their heads almost touching the ceiling, trying to decide what to do next. Si assured the children that rescue would come with the first light of morning. He got back in the water, grabbed the broom and broke out every window in the house. He told them that all the mud pouring in would hold down the house and that they would be safe. When he climbed back onto the table, he kept the broom with him, brushing at the water around their perch. The children soon realized that the broom kept them safe from snakes swimming in through the doors and windows.

Si and Hattie began praying. Si asked Hattie to forgive him for anything he might have done to hurt her during their life together. He instructed the children to always remember their religious training as they grew up. He kept talking to the children about what would happen when they escaped the flood and walked out to higher ground. His calm encouragement kept them from panicking.

Si looked at his watch and announced the time, almost 5:00 a.m. As he assured his family that first light and certain rescue were only minutes away, a wall of water about three feet high struck the house. The house shuddered and moved with the force of the water. For a short time, it rested against the water pump located on the east side of the house before the outer walls slipped out from under the roof.

Somehow, all the family managed to get out from under the roof and onto debris from the roof and walls. Si told the children to scramble onto the loosened doors and the roof, still floating in the rushing water. He helped Hattie to join Myrtle, Alfred and Rod on a piece of floating wall. He tried to boost Alta to join the rest of the family, but the wall tipped and swayed so much that he stopped. The wall did not seem to be strong enough to hold them all. Si quickly changed his mind, placing Alta on a different piece of floating wall. The river snatched her away from the rest of the family. When she looked back, Alta could see her father straddling the peak of the roof, waving goodbye.

Alta moved downstream, pulled along with the bodies of drowned cows, horses and cats for company. Even worse, live snakes and rats shared her fate. All were struggling to stay on the small piece of wall to escape the icy fingers of the river, steadily pulling them under. The river soon dumped Alta off her makeshift raft, causing her to go under the foul waters for a few

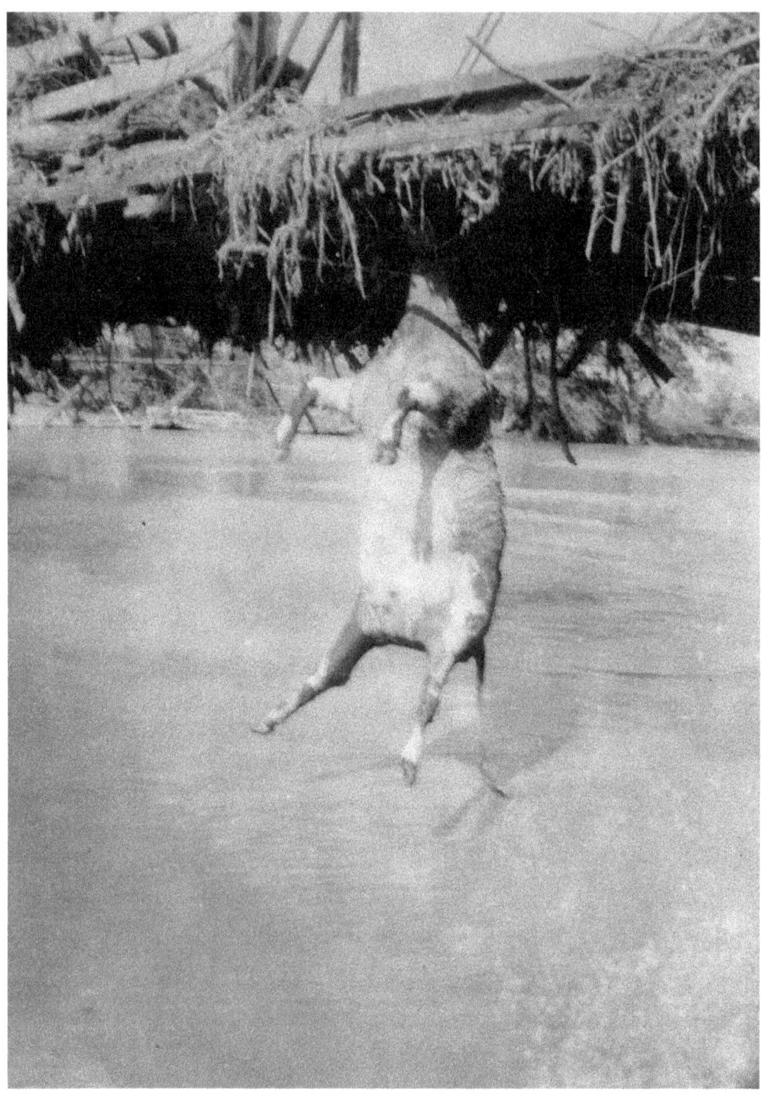

A cow caught by the horns. *Joseph Torrey.*

seconds. Unseen forces pulled her onward until she found herself across the river channel near a large cottonwood about two miles from her home's original location. She managed to climb into the tree. She remained there during the rest of her ordeal, trapped above the roaring flood. Within a few hours, Richard Delving and Art Whipple rescued her and carried her to their home to recover.

Myrtle, Alfred, Rod and their mother, Hattie, continued to struggle in the angry waves rushing on down the river. Hattie slipped off once. Myrtle grabbed Hattie by her hair and pulled her back onto the wall-turned-life-raft. As they sped on down the river, Myrtle reached up and caught hold of a tree. The wall tipped up with the shift in weight, and the rest of the family landed in the water.

Myrtle managed to stay in the tree, two and a half miles from where the house collapsed, on the north side of the river. During her imprisonment in the tree, a dust storm blew through the area. Adding to her distress, the sight of her brother Rod's body floating facedown in the water paralyzed her with fear. In shock from the trauma, she clung to the tree, unable to make a sound. Eric Lampe, John Leibbrandt and other neighbors finally spotted her at nightfall, reaching her as soon as the roaring water subsided enough to allow them to approach her precarious shelter with a homemade raft.

Meanwhile, Alfred came up under the wall of the house and managed to swim to a nearby tree. Some neighbors watching on the bank told him to let go and said they would throw him a rope and pull him to shore. This plan might have worked, but the tree collapsed before the rope could be tossed. The river took that opportunity to seize Alfred and sweep him out of their reach downstream.

The river then loosened its grasp, tossing him onto a small rise in the middle of the roaring water, where debris collected around a piece of farm equipment owned by Webb Scheller. Joining Alfred on the newly made island, an angry cow fought to stay out of the water, too. Alfred succeeded in avoiding the cow by hiding behind the machine. He saw a barn close to his island refuge near the riverbank. He heard men talking and working, but he could not hear what they said. The flood continued to gouge out a channel between Alfred and the barn. He cowered, afraid to move and too weak to cry out. Later, he discovered that although he could not call out loud enough to be heard, he could whistle. The men heard his whistling but at first could not see him. Finally, the men spotted him, but Alfred could not hear what they anxiously tried to tell him. The river kept his attention and seemed intent on keeping him a prisoner or drowning him along with his slim hope of rescue.

Alfred spent all day on the island in the river. As he grew colder and weaker, it seemed the river would claim him. As night fell, the men in the barn trained a spotlight on him to give him hope. Alfred slept fitfully in a hollow he dug in the debris to protect himself from the cold night air.

When he awoke the next morning, he was alone. Sometime in the night, the cow had abandoned him and the island of debris. Alfred could hear hammering in the barn but did not know until later that the men he had seen earlier had worked through the night building a raft to rescue him. Up for over forty-eight hours themselves, they worked steadily through the night to finish the raft. They used lumber and fifty-gallon barrels to design a raft tied with ropes. Later in the day, they completed the raft and carried it to the water.

The river still ran swift and deep, so some of the men held the raft with ropes on shore while others manned the raft as they tried to rescue Alfred. After several tries, they reached him and brought him over the angry water safely back to shore. During his ordeal, which lasted sixty hours, Alfred lost over nineteen pounds and suffered shock from exposure and dehydration. The seething river had carried him in its icy arms over three and a half miles downstream after tearing his home and family apart.

Friends listed Hattie, Rodney and Si among the missing and gave their descriptions to the authorities. The river abandoned Rodney's body about eighteen miles from his home; it was discovered by would-be rescuers searching for survivors.

Clara Magnani, who lived at the mouth of a canyon seven miles south of Benkelman, reported spotting Hattie clinging to a tree that was racing along in the angry river. Several days after Clara's report, two girls, Irene and Josephine Krug, bringing in the family's cows at milking time, saw a woman's shoe sticking out of some debris. On closer inspection, they realized it was attached to a dead body. They ran for help and described what they had found. The men who brought Hattie back to the Krug farm took a blanket to cover her, as the river had torn all her clothing from her body. The heartless river had taken her coat and three dresses, leaving only her tightly laced shoes.

Hattie's body waited for identification in a Benkelman barn that had been hastily converted into a morgue. When her older daughter, Blanche, came to identify her mother's body, Blanche shared with the family that she recognized her mother immediately. The river had bruised and battered her mother before finally inflicting a fatal blow, a wound in her head just above her temple. However, Hattie's long hair lay fanned all around her, still beautiful in spite of her ordeal.

Because the still-angry river made the return of Hattie's body to her family in Colorado impossible by land, she was wrapped with two white sheets as her shroud. A pilot gently tied her carefully prepared body to the wing of his small plane and flew her back to Hale. The family reunited Hattie and Rodney in a double funeral on June 5, 1935.

Cleanup crews found Si on June 25, 1935, buried in quicksand. His arm, raised above his head, had washed free, and some men clearing the river noticed his hand sticking out above the water. The men dug around him, changing the river's channel to retrieve his body. It is believed that Si walked out onto the riverbank after surviving the ride over the flood's powerful waters. He must not have noticed the quicksand, as he sank straight down into the waiting death trap and drowned. They found him with his clothing intact. His eyeglasses remained unbroken in the bib of his overalls pocket. Trapped near the shore, his body rested only half a mile from where workers found his son Rodney.

Residents reported that the crest of the flood appeared in Colorado as a wall of water approaching their homes. The river created this wall by picking up an incredible amount of debris. Like an angry Amazon bent on destruction, the river advanced. The debris became a deadly spearhead moving in advance of the rushing killer. Standing a reported five to twenty feet in height, depending on location, the wall of debris brought terror to all in its path. In front of the wall, terrified wildlife, including hundreds of rabbits, ran until they dropped from exhaustion, unable to escape. From the safety of high ground, people watched this exodus. In most cases, the river overtook and drowned everything in its path.

The river's waters changed as it advanced. Before the storm, the river ran clear, shallow and beautiful. Now it took on a different, evil character—that of a powerful, yellow, foul-smelling, freezing soup filled with the living and the dying.

Those fighting for their lives in the water battled fence wire, topsoil, animals, portions of buildings crushed by the water, farm implements—literally everything that lay in the river's path. The river helped itself to all the topsoil as it raced across the dry and barren land, leaving behind a deposit of fine, worthless sand unfit for growing crops.

Irven Wengert reported that his family owned a field of wheat they hoped to salvage. When they attempted to cut the crop, they found the ground covered in debris, including a beehive, auto tires and parts of the nearby recreation area, making it impossible to harvest the grain.

Chapter 6

Kansas Taken by Surprise

In St. Francis, Kansas, Ben Parks woke to the sound of tramping hooves. When he looked outside, he saw cattle moving through town ahead of the floodwaters. Lightning flashes revealed the street slipping beneath the widening floodwaters. The river, under the cover of roaring thunder and vivid lightning, crept into town and trapped people in their homes while they slept. It eventually rose to fifteen feet above its normal flow.

A second and much noisier wave of flooding entered the community at about 7:00 a.m. At that time, Oscar Ferguson found himself trapped at the City Light Plant. Carl Stone, with the aid of a rope secured on the bank by Lester Confer, rescued Oscar from a watery death. Lights all over town went out. The city remained without electricity for over a week as the river took its time receding. Afterward, it took days to clean the plant of mud and debris left by the slovenly river.

A crowd gathered at the water's edge to watch as the flood roared past. A shout went out at about 8:30 a.m. as homes started to float away on the west side of town. As they watched in amazement, a house swirled down the river right in front of startled onlookers. It came to a temporary rest, bumping gently into the shoreline. The door opened, and out popped the Jake Rogers family, each carrying a few of their belongings. They jumped to shore without getting their feet wet. As if propelled by unseen hands, the house moved away again. The door stood open, and a lighted kerosene lamp stood steady on the table inside. The house sped up as the river moved it along more quickly. The crowd watched in horror as the river, assured by

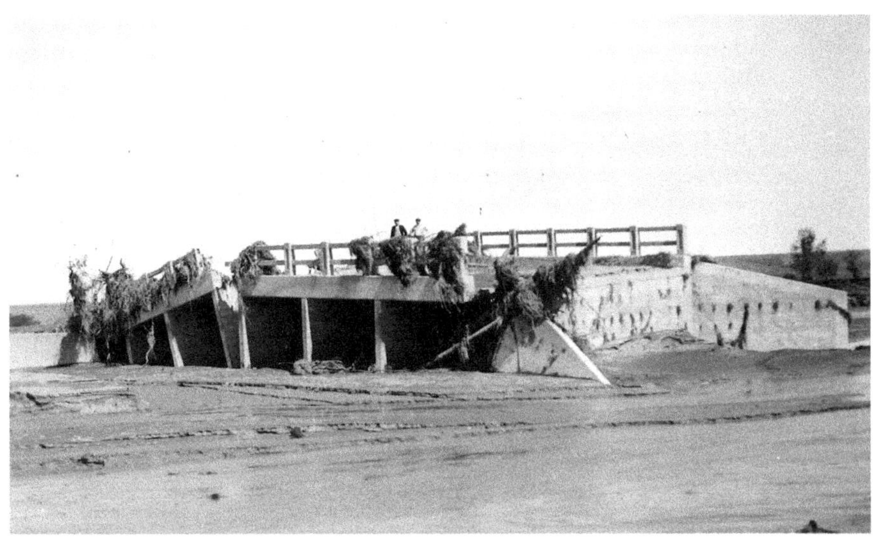

A bridge with no road in St. Francis, Kansas, after the flood. *Cheyenne County Museum.*

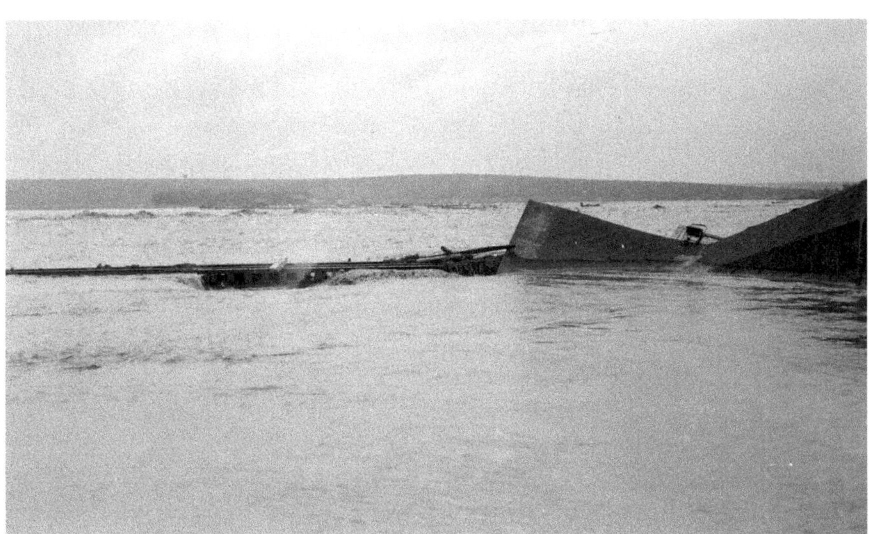

A destroyed bridge near St. Francis, Kansas. *Cheyenne County Museum.*

now of the onlookers' full attention, plucked up the house and dashed it to pieces against other debris already gathered in the river.

Betty Harrison Miller, who lived near St. Francis, remembered her mother waking the family on the night of the flood. Mrs. Harrison told them she woke because she smelled the flood coming before she heard the roar of the water. The entire family got up and dressed quickly, ready to flee if necessary. At first light, they realized the wrathful river, under cover of darkness, had sliced their farm in two. The South Fork of the Republican now ran in a different course, its angry waters tearing away anything unable to flee from its wrath. The trapped family watched in horror as huge cottonwood trees tumbled like thistles in a windstorm as the river washed away the soil around their roots.

Weeks passed before the family could leave the farm. All roads and bridges in or out of their area vanished with the onslaught of angry water. Betty's father drove through the fields to an area where a neighbor met him in a low spot in the new riverbed. The neighbor waited for him to cross and gave him a ride into town. The men purchased supplies for their families and then returned over the same laborious route.

Irene Barnhart lost her life when the flood hit her family's rural St. Francis home. She lost her footing as the family moved to higher ground. The hostile waves forced her against a fence, ensnaring her legs with debris. After the floodwaters receded, Irene's body remained trapped, wedged in the fence.

The river destroyed many rural Kansas homes. Fields polished clean stood devoid of all topsoil. Piles of debris remained as monuments to the flood's bloody rampage. Many families, already pushed to the edge of disaster by the drought and the Depression, could not recover from the total devastation of their homes and farming operations. The land, only the day before fertile and full of promise from recent gentle rain, turned into a worthless investment

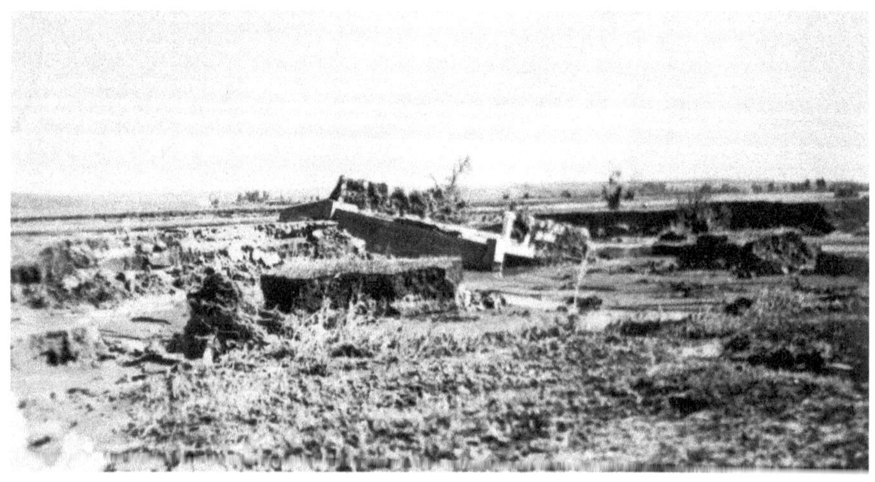

Debris left by the receding river near St. Francis, Kansas. *Cheyenne County Museum.*

in sand and water. Others were devastated by the fickle Republican's change in channel, with their farms now completely under water.

Farmers and townspeople faced the daunting task of cleanup as floodwaters receded. Piles of debris not only held the dead but also teemed with poisonous snakes, making cleanup dangerous work. The treacherous quicksand, left behind in holes dug by the violent river, quickly swallowed unwary men and animals. The body of Clarence Lothian, one of the first victims to be swept away by the swollen river near his home in Seibert, Colorado, resurfaced in one of these dangerous debris piles. Checking fences on her land, Hettie Galvin made the grisly discovery along the west edge of the river. Clarence's clothes hooked around a fencepost during the flood. Hettie discovered him almost a month after he drowned on June 28, 1935.

Residents of St. Francis searched in vain for the new bridge on Highway 36. It had disappeared forever, gobbled up by the hungry river. According to the history of the flood published by the Cheyenne County Historical Society, the bridge was later discovered when the construction crew building a replacement found a portion of the old bridge deck buried under forty feet of sand.

Chapter 7

ENTERING NEBRASKA

A cubic foot of water is approximately 7.48 gallons, or 8.34 pounds. Cubic feet per second is the measure of water moving by a specified location across the entire channel of a river or other body of water. The Republican River picked up speed as more and more rain fell and the elevation decreased. In an inspection following the flood, surveyors estimated that up to 260,000 cubic feet per second of water had moved down the Republican at Bloomington, Nebraska. Flood stories of tragedy and heroism occurred over and over in Nebraska along the once-placid river. The names changed from town to town, but catastrophes reoccurred countless times, each remarkably similar.

HAIGLER

Jack Miller drove his truck through the hills along the river on the highway near Haigler at about the time the river began to rise in the early morning hours of May 31, 1935, according to the *Benkelman Post*. He remembered that the oppressive air made it very difficult to breathe. After he crossed the bridge across the Arikaree, he saw the Republican River roaring across the

Opposite, top: A car destroyed by the flood near Benkelman, Nebraska. *Lucille Edwards*.

Opposite, bottom: The Crest Discharge Report. *Follansbee and Spiegel Report*.

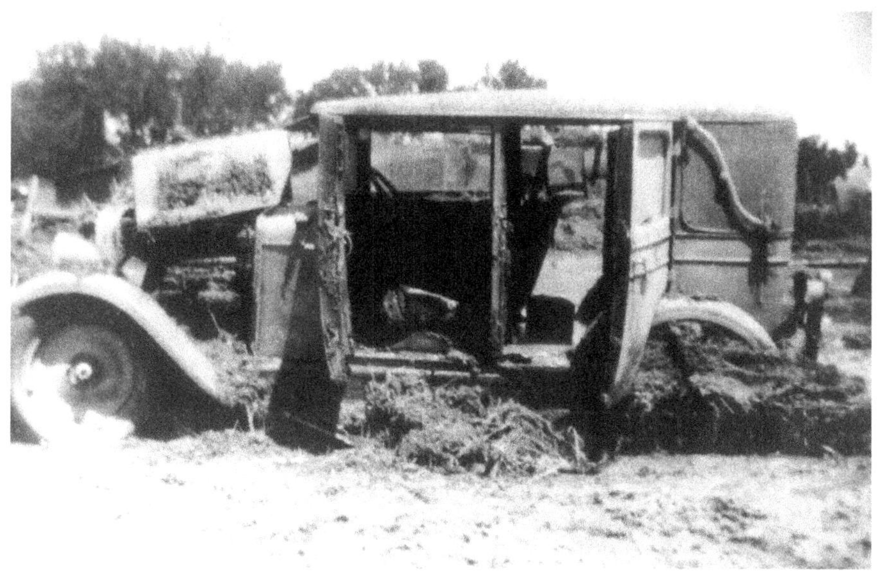

Crest discharge of the flood of May-June 1935 at points along the valley of the Republican and Kansas Rivers.

Place	Drainage area (square miles)	Crest discharge (second-feet) Total	Per square mile
Arikaree River:			
Cope, Colo.	690	25,000	36.2
North of Idalia, Colo.	1,190	54,000	45.4
Haigler, Nebr.	1,600	50,000	31.2
South Fork of Republican River:			
Newton, Colo.	1,270	103,000	81.1
Kansas-Nebraska line	2,550	150,000	58.8
Republican River:			
Max, Nebr.	7,740	190,000	*32.5
McCook	12,000	245,000	**24.0
Cambridge (below Medicine Creek)	14,200	280,000	‡22.8
Bloomington	20,900	260,000	12.4
Hardy	22,410	225,000	10.0
Scandia, Kans.	22,930	215,000	9.4
Clay Center	24,570	195,000	7.9
Junction City (above Smoky Hill River)	24,960	168,000	6.7
Kansas River:			
Junction City (below Smoky Hill River)	44,910	179,000	4.0
Ogden	45,240	170,000	3.8
Manhattan:			
Above Big Blue River	45,470	160,000	3.5
Below Big Blue River	55,070	190,000	3.4
Wamego	55,240	177,000	3.2
Topeka	56,710	154,000	2.7
Lecompton	58,420	144,000	2.5
Bonner Springs	59,890	122,000	2.0
Kansas City	60,060	120,000	2.0

* The net area contributing to the flood and used in computing discharge per square mile at Max, Nebr., was 5,840 square miles.

** The net area contributing to the flood and used in computing discharge per square mile at McCook, Nebr., was 10,200 square miles.

‡ The net area contributing to the flood and used in computing discharge per square mile at Cambridge, Nebr., was 12,300 square miles.

highway in the valley below, so he stopped his truck. He set his brakes and waited for the water to recede.

Instead, the water continued to rise, five inches in only ten minutes. Soon it reached the truck and came up through the floorboards. Waves slammed against the cab, causing the water to spray to the ceiling. Debris settled around the vehicle, and the truck started to move. Jack felt the truck being drawn toward the deep water by the angry river, which rushed higher and drew closer with each passing minute.

Using a stick to push away debris from the door, he gained access to the truck bed. He fought to push away the ever-increasing mounds piled relentlessly around the truck by the evil river threatening to swamp his truck. He fought this lonely battle all night long.

During his struggle, Jack considered leaping onto a large tree floating by. He was prepared to jump when lightning lit the sky, and he saw the tree swirl away in a violent whirlpool. It moved away from the truck and out of his reach. His despair turned to relief, however, when he saw the tree dashed against a mound of debris, shooting the massive trunk over fifteen feet in the air. He watched in horror as the river then sucked the mangled tree under, spewing it out again fifty yards farther downstream. Jack felt weak with relief that he chose not to jump into such a violent, watery grave.

While he waited, the Burlington Number Six, a passenger train called the Aristocrat, went by slowly on the tracks near the highway. Men on a handcar preceded the train, testing the track. Jack watched in amazement as the train passed along after the handcar. As the train proceeded slowly, the track sagged visibly into the floodwaters. As the last train car moved over the railroad bridge, the track disappeared into the flood.

Jack remained trapped on his truck until well after daylight. Soaked to the skin and deafened by the roar of the water, he waited for the water to recede. He finally braved the still-rushing water and walked to higher ground to search for help. He returned later in the day and, with help from a man with a Caterpillar tractor, dug his truck from the debris.

Parks

The flood also struck Parks, Nebraska, during the night. Dorothy Burke, a sweet-faced brunette, told the following story to a WPA worker who documented her tragic story:

We lived in Parks, the first house south of the Post Office. We had two children then. Our little boy was one year old and five months and Lois was three and five months. She was the child lost in the flood. I guess it was about 4:00 a.m.—about daylight—when it had been raining right along. My husband thought he'd get up, and then said he couldn't work because it had been raining so bad.

We then heard somebody knock at the door and heard them holler something. They said, "Something's coming." But we didn't understand what they meant was coming. My husband jumped up and looked out and said, "Oh, Dorothy, we're surrounded with water!" I thought he was joking so I didn't get up just then. Then when I did I was scared and began getting dressed. Lois came in then; she'd heard us and gotten out of her little bed. I held her up to the window and my husband said, "Oh don't do that. You'll scare her." He got his overalls on and I just got stockings on and a coat over my gown. I put a sweater and jacket on Lois. I took the baby and he had the little girl.

We tried to get out, but the water was so strong we couldn't hardly get the door open. When we did, we saw a man with three little boys trying to cross the street and the boy's heads were just above the water. We were intending to cross the highway and north to some houses on higher ground. But when we got to the highway where the water was so strong—we hadn't thought about the main current coming down the road right through town—I couldn't keep my feet. So we went with the current to a filling station on the north side of the road going east out of town.

There were three oil pumps at this filling station. We went between the two west ones...We had thought we would go into the oil station, but got half-way from the pumps to the door. My husband said, "Look what's coming!" I looked up and saw a rick of old railroad ties floating and tumbling toward us. We dodged back behind a pump. When the rick hit the pumps it broke them apart. I had to keep them...away from me. I had the baby in one arm and was bent over pushing the ties away. They kept swirling around me in an eddy.

I looked up to see where he was and he was on his back, and the water was eddying so, and he had dropped Lois. One of the ties from the rick had went under the water and came up and hit him. He fell and lost her. I tried to grab her dress and failed, and grabbed for her hair and she got away from me. I called him and told him she had gotten away. I told him to get her. I looked and she was screaming for help.

When she got to about the third pump she got up. She wasn't crying—she looked at me with her pretty blue eyes. Then it seemed like a wall of water was just behind her. As it caught her she threw up her hands. I was screaming. Some men heard me. My husband went after her...He tried again and again, but each time she was just ahead of him. There was a funnel of mist where the creek joined the river and I knew God had taken little sister. By this time my husband had been swept under the water...When he came up he could just reach the bridge (where the creek joins the Republican River) with his fingers. He had a terrible struggle but finally got up there and hung to the bridge, and that was all he could do.

While I was there at that oil pump, with my arm through that hose and holding the baby, dead animals, buildings, and pieces of buildings and everything you could mention came down the current past me and around me. It was so cold—the baby was cold and I was exhausted. I thought I'd go to the house. I got maybe four feet and was carried off my feet. There was nothing to get hold of—but a telephone wire came into my reach just like magic and with its help I got swept back to the pump where I hung on.

I was afraid Archie would be lost from the bridge, the water was pouring over it so. I was standing with my back to the pump, with my arm through the gas hose, holding the baby. I prayed...and it seemed my prayer was answered so easy. Three men had gotten a long stick to help them avoid the holes and were there beside me before I knew it. I had been there for four and a half hours...They didn't say anything. I think they were afraid...One of them took the baby and they helped me. I was almost past walking, I'd stayed there so long. I was crying and telling them about the little girl we'd lost. They got a rope and threw it to my husband. They were afraid to go to the bridge for fear it would give way. He got the rope and they pulled him in and brought him to where I was and put us both to bed.

A man came in from west of town with a team and wagon to get people out. They took us away. We stayed there until the flood went down. We couldn't find her little body and never have found it. But lots of people hunted for it.

Like the Burkes, the people of Parks lost almost everything in the flood. Before the flood, the little town had boasted two grocery stores, a hotel, a lumberyard and a gas station. The river destroyed or moved all but two of the town's buildings and left most filled with filthy water, making cleanup a monumental task.

Despite the loss of her sister, Mary Pettit, Mrs. Tom Ballard opened her home to the community. For over a week, with the help of neighbors, she set up a tent and served meals to as many as two hundred people in the Parks community. Parks never really recovered. Those who lived there wanted to be on higher ground, and most never returned to the once-thriving community.

BENKELMAN

Warned by the crew of the Burlington Number Six train, a call went out from Burlington Railroad agent G.P.B. Towle at 1:00 a.m. warning Benkelman of the coming flood. He also phoned residents in the southern parts of town and on the south side of the river, advising them to get to higher ground. Modern transportation proved useless, as roads and bridges washed away. Railroad tracks turned on end like giant picket fences. No supplies came into the area for many days. Families survived with no communication with the outside world and no way to learn about the safety of loved ones not at home when the flood began.

The flood devastated the community. Living so near the Republican, hundreds became trapped as they slept. Whole families vanished into eternity. The flood began at 3:00 a.m. on May 31. The water continued to

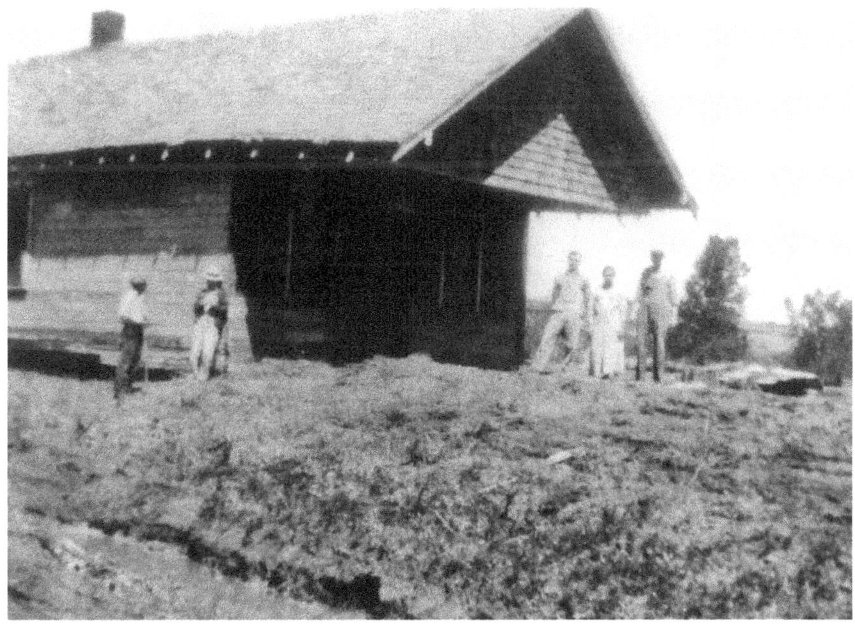

Unidentified home near Benkelman, Nebraska. *Lucille Edwards.*

rise and fall as the first and second crests tore through town at 9:00 a.m. and again at 3:30 p.m. The water spread to three and a half miles in width and reached a depth of twenty feet in the river channels. Observers measured waves over fourteen feet high at the point where the North and South Forks meet with Big Timber Creek.

Those who lost their lives included Peter Courtright, Ora Davis, Art Duvall, the Faylor family (including Bert; his wife, Jennie; Bert Jr.; and Merna), Mrs. Robert Harrison, Joanna Osborne, the Pettit family (including James, Mary Isabelle, Albert, Thomas, Edward, James, LaVeta and Lee), John Sandgran, George Taylor and his family of four and Myrna Workman.

The Aristocrat, the fastest train on the Burlington Railroad route, rolled in to Benkelman just as the tracks vanished behind it. Passengers from Denver bound for New Jersey found themselves marooned in the small Nebraska town. By the time the flood ended, 1,332 miles of Burlington track would be affected by the disaster. It would be forty-five days before normal schedules resumed and the train moved out of town.

First light on the morning of May 31, 1935, revealed a raging sea of water lapping at the railroad ties. Local townspeople lined up along the tracks, looking south at the devastation. Some people owned spyglasses, which they used to spot victims clinging in trees. They watched helplessly as a man on a makeshift raft screamed for help as his rickety craft raced downriver. From high ground, they saw the channel of the river change. The railroad tracks east of town had washed out, and rails and ties stood together like a twisted fence.

Frantic railroad passengers anxious to notify their families of their location relied on a kind ham radio operator, Roy Olmsted, W9FA, who relayed messages to their family members assuring them of their safety. The marooned travelers would eventually be driven by automobile to a Union Pacific line eighty-five miles north in Ogallala, Nebraska.

Many who escaped to higher ground returned to find their homes completely destroyed. Some homes disappeared entirely as the angry river quickly tore them apart. The river picked the structures up like dollhouses and abandoned them in neighboring fields. Homes of stone or concrete fared better but still filled with mud and debris—often as high as the second story.

Josephine "Jo" Krug Mann lived in one of these concrete houses. She recalled her excitement when it rained on May 30. Her father, Joe, told her mother, "Well, Mama, we're going to get a rain and save our crops!" About 5:00 a.m. on May 31, they received a line ring on their phone, the 1935 version of reverse 911. Everyone answered when they heard this ring because it signaled an emergency in the area.

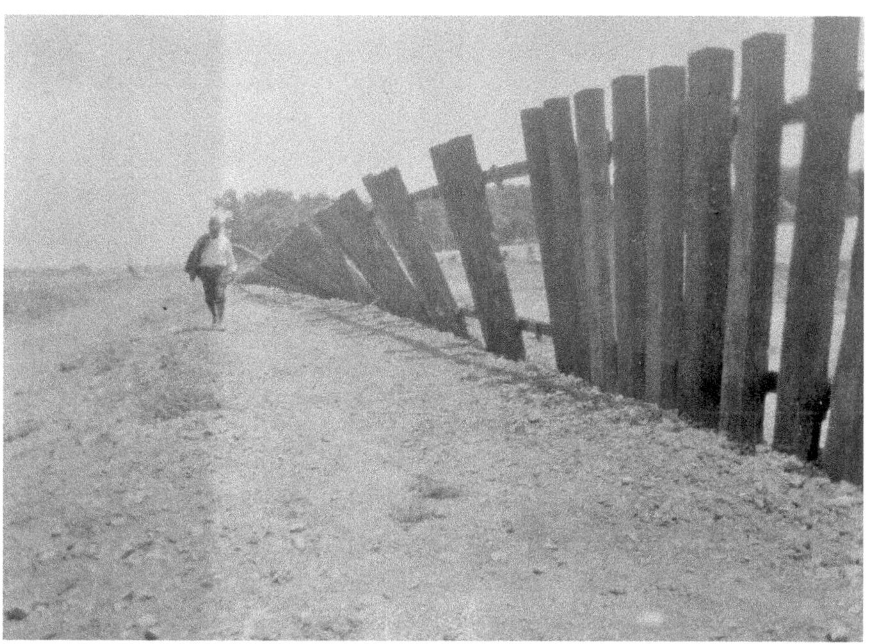

Twisted railroad ties near Alma, Nebraska. *Joseph Torrey*.

The operator said that everyone living on the river bottom must get to higher ground because a terrible flood was approaching. Jo's father did not believe the water could get as high as their house, even though the North and South Forks of the Republican joined in their adjoining pasture just south of Benkelman. He said they would stay at home.

A few minutes later, another call passed along the rumor of a dam giving way in Colorado. Meanwhile, the massive amount of rain deposited upriver earlier in the evening rushed their way. The family stayed put, but they began to hear people screaming for help. When they went outside their home, they saw all kinds of things going down the river. Joe rushed to free wooden gates from his fences, hoping trapped neighbors might use them as rafts and reach the safety of the high ground.

The Krug family placed great value in their farm operation. They could not afford to lose their cattle, an important part of their income. In addition, they raised other animals for food, including chickens and ducks. To protect newly hatched baby chicks and ducks, Jo's mother placed them inside the kitchen in washtubs—chicks in one tub and ducks in the other.

At about 7:00 a.m., the local police came to the Krugs' home and told them they had to move to high ground. The family, including Joe, Jo, her elder sister Irene and her mother, Bertha, loaded into their car and headed for town. Just as the family crossed the bridge, it collapsed. The roaring river turned it upside down and swept it away.

Everyone in town assembled at Druliner Hill. Joe worried about his fat cattle, so important to the family's livelihood. Although everyone begged him not to, he borrowed a horse from the livestock sale barn and plunged the animal into the flood. He planned to cut the barbed-wire fences around his pastures so that the cattle would not be trapped and drown wedged against them. Joe understood, as did hundreds of other farmers along the river, how a fence could quickly become a death trap, entangling livestock. It could also become a barrier behind which debris would build until the whole mass would be sent downstream to lodge against another obstacle, compounding the force of the wall of water with each barrier it overpowered in the rush downriver.

The family could see Joe go under shortly after he entered the water, but his horse kept swimming. A few minutes later, someone shouted that he saw Joe hanging on the side of the horse. Joe, even with hands badly cut by barbed wire, managed to save his cattle. With the help of a railroad crew five miles downriver, he fought his way onto the shore and out of the river's clutches.

Jo remembered opening the dresser drawers in their bedrooms when they returned home. She found them filled to the brim with mud. The flood had reached as high as the fourth step of their two-story home. The kitchen suffered the most damage, as the river left a terrible mess of slime and debris. The baby chicks lay drowned in their washtub, but the ducks swam happily in the ruined kitchen.

The family rejoiced when they finally learned that their son and brother, Henry, living on their farm ten miles upstream, remained safe. He told them he awoke to the terrible roar of the wild water. He walked outside to see for himself the result of the storm. Seeing the power of the river filled him with terror for his family as he imagined them trapped in their home on the river bottom.

The Krug family did feel blessed that they survived, as neighbors on both sides of them died in the flood. Their neighbors the Pettit family went into the attic of their home. Friends attempted a rescue, swimming out to the house during the early stages of the flood. However, Robbin Pettit feared the weaker members of the family could not swim out, so he decided the entire family would stay together and wait out the flood. When the first crest of the flood hit their home, the wall of water consumed the house, which disappeared under the waves. Following the flood, rescuers searched the wreckage of the home. They found the Pettits, all their bodies lying close together, in the home's three-foot attic space.

The Faylor family lived on the opposite side of the Krugs. Their home stood clear of all previous flood high-water marks at the end of a long curve in the river, close to the riverbank. Surrounded by large trees, some over seventy-five years old, the home seemed to be the focus of the approaching floodwaters. The river blasted a new channel directly through its location.

Witnesses reported seeing lights in the upstairs windows of the Faylor house. They heard Jennie Faylor scream as a wall of water battered their home. The house exploded, and the debris scattered in the rushing water. Later, neighbors found small items belonging to the Faylors, but the river never gave up their bodies. Bert Faylor raised strawberry roan horses, and the neighbors did see the stallion swim free of the barn. The horse was found later. A portion of the manger still hung from the horse's halter. Three of the family's mares also reappeared downriver.

The Faylors' adult sons—Harry, George and Chuck—spent weeks looking in every side canyon, searching every possible spot where their family's bodies might have lodged. Neighbors believed the river used a gravel pit located near their home as a grave. They speculated that the river deposited them and their home deep in the pit in a subterranean tomb, covering all evidence of their existence with sand and debris. Neighbors and friends dug in the pit for many days searching for their bodies, but the river buried them deep and hid them well. Even though they found small debris from the Faylor home in the pit, such as a pitchfork with Bud's initials on it and a lap robe, larger items such as the piano and the family car were never found.

Many families became separated by the flood. As travel and communications ceased in the valley, those with family living near the river worried constantly, not knowing the fate of their loved ones.

The Peter O'Brien family, who lived south of Benkelman, experienced this in a very agonizing way. Peter, his wife and their three eldest sons traveled north to Imperial, Nebraska, to spend Memorial Day. They left their eldest daughter, eighteen-year-old Mary, at home to care for their younger children. When they returned south, they discovered floodwaters blocking their path home. Frantic with fear, they knew their farm had most likely flooded during their absence.

Terrified for the safety of their children, and unable to merely stand and wait, the family decided to drive around the flood. They drove to Fort Morgan, Colorado, and angled cross-county over 200 miles west, connecting with Highway 24 and returning east to Goodland, Kansas. From there, they traveled north to Bird City, Kansas, and then hurried home. They left Benkelman at about noon on Friday and did not reach home until Sunday afternoon.

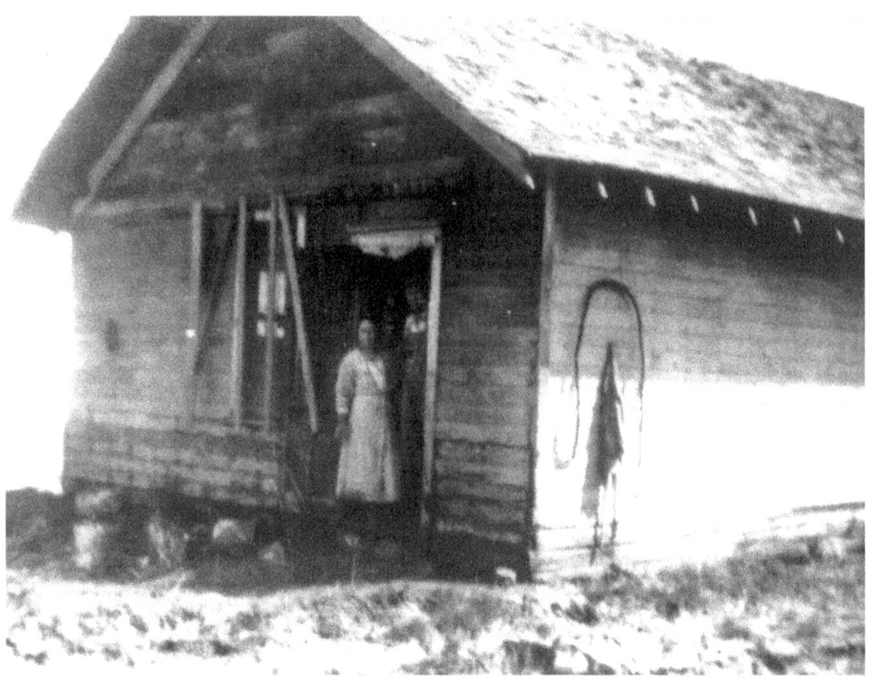

Damaged home near Benkelman, Nebraska. *Lucille Edwards.*

A joyful reunion took place near their home, which was surrounded by water but still stood. The children stayed safe, thanks to their thoughtful neighbors and the good judgment of eldest daughter, Mary. The O'Briens' journey resulted in a happy ending. Hundreds of other families did not share their good fortune.

Max

The river wiped Max, Nebraska, almost totally off the map. Except for one concrete-walled filling station, everything else was stolen by the angry river. The river's first crest reached Max at 9:45 a.m. with a height of 11.8 feet above flood stage. It fell gradually until the second crest reached the community at 2:00 p.m. The river reached 11.2 feet with an overflow of 4,000 feet in width.

Stratton

Heavy rain fell all day in Stratton on Friday, May 31, 1935. Later, residents estimated that at least eight inches had fallen in their area. Families gathered on the bluffs overlooking the river to view the debris. They saw animals being swept downstream by the swirling waters. They watched to see if their neighbors on the other side of the river had reached safety. Some, like the Stonecipher family, did not. At home that day were Alva and Myrtle Stonecipher; their teenage son, Cleo; their twin daughters, Hildred and Mildred; and their niece, Ethel Black. The Stonecipher place stood in the direct path of the advancing wall of water, estimated at some twenty feet in height and racing down the valley.

As the water began to rise, Cleo and his father went out to look after the cattle. Cleo saw the danger and tried to get away from the rapidly approaching high water on horseback. He finally abandoned his horse and managed to make his way to the roof of their barn, where he waited out the flood and hoped for rescue.

The rest of his family made their way to the roof of the house, awaiting rescue. As the water rose and the current became stronger, the house came loose from its foundation and began to float with the current. As it floated, it began to tip and slanted so much that the family struggled to hang on. One mile downstream, the house came to a stop against some trees blocking its path, near where Camp Creek enters the Republican. At this point, the Stoneciphers still clung to the safety of the roof.

Few boats existed in southwest Nebraska in the 1930s, none motorized. When the Stoneciphers began their journey atop their house, rescuers did not have a way to help them. Hours passed before two men, Frank Bowland and Reasoner Burden, obtained a rescue boat and made their first attempt to reach the family as they perched precariously on the roof of the house.

Four times the boat swept past the house. The river's current fought with the men, making it impossible to bring the boat close enough to take anyone from the roof. Each time the pair tried and failed, they landed downstream, where a neighbor's truck brought them back upstream for another try. Finally, the men attached a rope to their boat and secured it to the truck on shore. This time they made contact with the people on the roof.

Afraid they might not be able to repeat a second rescue, they loaded all five of the stranded family members into the boat and set out to attempt a landing downstream. Seven people aboard the small boat made it much more difficult to maneuver. With the added weight of the rescued people,

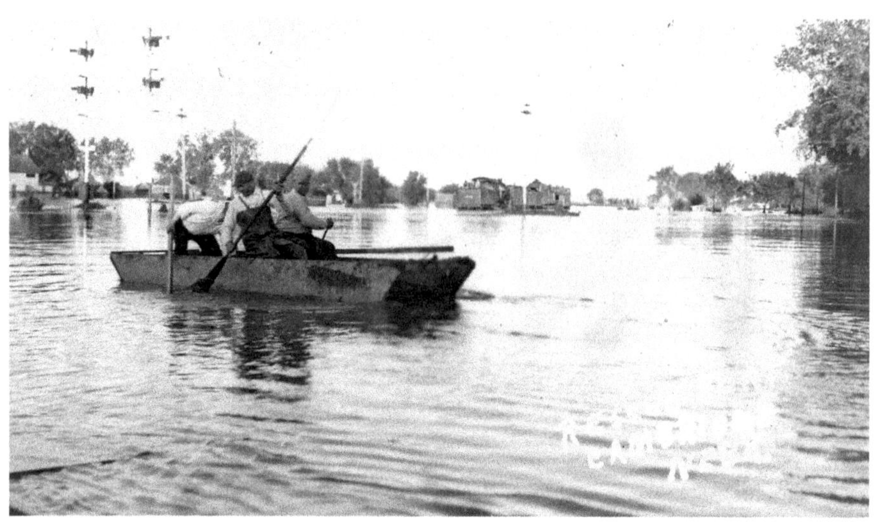

This rescue boat was built on the night of the flood and launched at 6:00 a.m. the next day. *Cambridge Museum.*

the rope snapped. The river pounced on this opportunity, sucking them all downstream and into even more danger.

The boat, with the would-be rescuers still clinging to their oars, came to a spot in the river where trees and debris had become lodged in a railroad bridge tossed aside by the killer waves. This formed a sort of dam and created a waterfall in the river. The men at the oars fought valiantly with the river, trying to steer around the obstacle. Instead, they went over the waterfall. The boat capsized, and everyone landed in the water. The two boatmen clung to the damaged hull of the boat. However, the river picked them up and carried them downstream. The men finally wrenched themselves from the river's grasp and made their way to the shore and safety.

Myrtle; her niece, Ethel; and Mildred were swept away by the river and drowned. Alva and Hildred managed to cling to debris but remained several yards from the shore. Too exhausted to try to make landfall, they held on, in constant peril of being dislodged from their hazardous perch by floating debris.

On the shore, neighbor Bill Campbell, his sons and a few of the neighbor boys worked frantically to take another rope to Alva and Hildred and bring them to shore. After a number of attempts, they succeeded in reaching the pair. With the help of eight to ten boys pulling on the rope, Alva and his daughter reached safety. Cleo, still on the barn at the farm, survived his lonely ordeal and was later reunited with the surviving members of his family.

TRENTON

The flood, roaring like hundreds of freight trains coming down the tracks, hit Trenton between 4:00 and 5:00 a.m. on May 31. At about 7:00 a.m., the bridge over the river was swept away. Rain kept up steadily all day, and another heavy downpour from the northwest fell at about 2:00 p.m. This contributed to Trenton being one of the towns most affected by the flood.

Telephone operators in Trenton did not leave their posts until the floodwaters began to surge in the backdoor of their office. Ella Spangler and Lillie Taylor finally left their posts when a boat came to take them to safety. They called and pleaded with the river bottom residents to take their livestock and families to high ground. They kept at it, at about fifteen-minute intervals, until the advancing river snapped all remaining telephone lines.

Many residents refused to be alarmed. Others, fearing the town would completely wash away, spent the day and the following night on the hills north of town. Panic increased when the rain filled the creeks and canyons north of town, causing water to rush by on all sides in its maddening race to join the Republican.

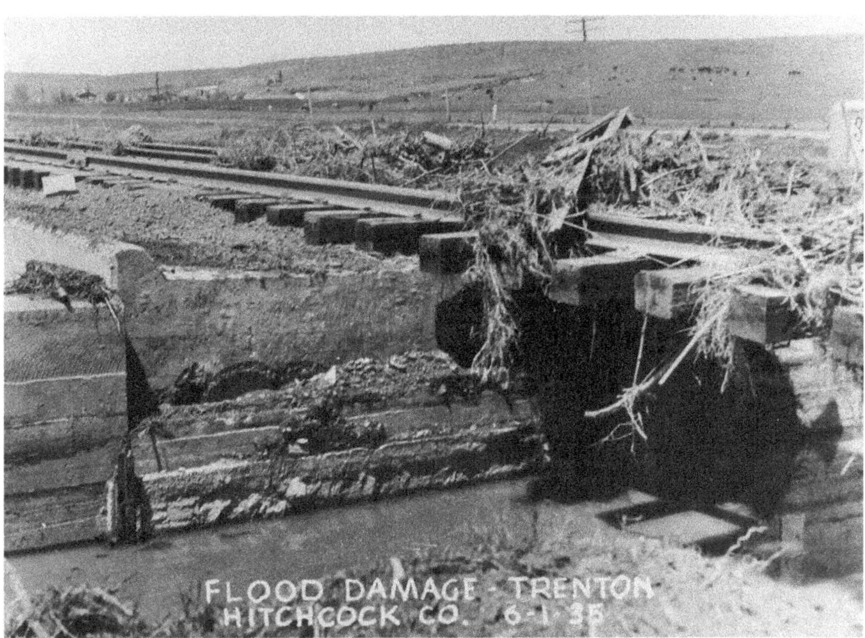

Flood damage near Trenton, Nebraska. *Mary Sherk.*

As water filled the local jail, Trenton sheriff Lynn Campbell freed prisoner Norman Herrick, held there on suspicion of illegally breaking and entering. When Herrick exited the jail, he saw a dog trapped in a tree in mid-river. Without a thought for his own safety, Herrick jumped into the roiling waters, swam one hundred yards and rescued the terrified animal.

Trenton suffered the loss of many of its citizens. The dead included Clark Colver and his seven-year-old-son, George; Owen Murtha and his wife, Nora; Howard Smith and his wife; and James Thomas and his wife, Mary, and son Spencer. Mary's body was found over seventy-five miles away, hung from the branches of a tall tree near Edison, Nebraska.

Joe Fleming, who lived near Trenton, watched as what seemed like a whole lumberyard came down the river. Bundles of shingles, rolls of corn cribbing, all kinds of lumber and even whole buildings swept past as he and his family watched in horror. Later, they learned that the contents of the St. Francis, Kansas lumber store, located about forty-five miles upstream, had passed by them, carried away by the bandit river.

J.W. "Bill" Rogers, age sixty-five, worked for Guy Mollison on his stock farm two miles east of Trenton. Mollison's shepherd dog was also often at the farm. At about 6:00 a.m. on May 31, 1935, Rogers, accompanied by the dog, went to do the chores at the barn, which stood quite a distance from the house. There, he fed horses, cattle and hogs. He noticed the river rising and water rapidly approaching the barn, so he hurried to complete his duties. As he came out of the barn, he discovered that the river had crept silently all around the barn while he was working inside. Worried about the animals trapped inside, he hurried back to set them free. Looking outside, he saw the river swell in a wave two to three feet in height as he hurried to release the horses. He freed them just as a second swell, three to four feet high, swept him and the livestock away.

Rogers caught hold of a wire fence and struggled to pull himself to a tree and safety. The river dashed him against a large elm tree. It pulled him under as he fought to reach the safety of the tree's branches, sometimes completely submerging him. Rogers managed to hold on to the wire and finally reached a lower limb of the tree.

The shepherd dog struggled to stay with Rogers, who pulled the dog into the tree with him. One of the barn cats soon joined them as well. Rogers and the animals remained in the tree as the water rushed around them. At about 2:00 p.m., the barn collapsed with a loud crash, and the river carried it away. While he and the animals watched, the entire farmstead disappeared, tugged along by the swollen river with only the tree where they crouched left standing. They watched the annihilation of over half of the farm as the river chewed it up and swept it away.

It continued to rain very hard, soaking Rogers, the dog and the cat. Rogers shivered so much that it became hard for him to maintain a grip on the tree as he crouched on the precarious safety of a fragile limb. In response to Roger's distress, the dog settled himself around Roger's shoulders like a shawl. The cat curled into his lap. Together they waited and watched for the murderous river to recede. Encouraged by the warmth from the animals, Rogers clung to the branch with renewed energy. Meanwhile, neighbors spotted Rogers in the tree at about 4:00 p.m. They came as close as they dared, remaining on the high ground near the farmstead.

The men on the riverbank pointed the lights of their cars on Rogers and the animals so they would not feel alone waiting there in the dark. At about 10:00 p.m., the water went down to about five feet in depth. Rogers felt his body growing weaker. He realized he could not hold on much longer. He lowered himself into the water and set out for land. Abandoned by the cat, Rogers and the dog began the treacherous trip to dry land with shouts of encouragement from the men on high ground. The river, though less swift and strong, left a minefield of debris and quicksand to block the pair's path to safety.

The dog took the lead, helping Rogers to shore. Rogers followed the dog using a six-foot stick he found to ward off debris. With much hard work and patience, the dog led Rogers over half a mile to safety. At times, both the man and the dog waded or crawled as the dog sniffed out a path for Rogers around the quicksand to the shoreline. By the time he reached dry land, Rogers collapsed from exhaustion. His clothes, filled with sticks, mud and trash, dragged him down. He credited the dog with saving his life as he reached the arms of waiting rescuers.

CULBERTSON

Floodwaters reached Culbertson at the same time the Frenchman and Blackwood Creeks overflowed their banks. The combined overflow reached a width of over two miles at its peak and raced through the southern portion of the community. Bystanders on the high ground above the river watched in horror as the river picked up and carried away the home of the Wallace family, with the entire family still inside. Other witnesses downstream near

Blackwood Creek watched in shock as the river dashed the Wallace house to bits. Abducted by the river, none of the family survived. They included Bernard "Red" Wallace; his wife, Delores; and children Virginia, Martha Jean, Bernice and Lorraine.

Chapter 8

On to McCook

Lloyd Harvey, a driver for the Johnson Fruit Company, drove home on the evening of May 30, 1935, in the pouring rain, unaware of the destruction the flood's impact was bringing with it. He lived with his family in a home on the west side of McCook, where he could look outside and see the valley stretching out in both directions. When he went out the next morning to take a look around and scan the valley, evidence of the storm's impact could be seen everywhere. Herds of livestock gathered on high ground. Many roads disappeared under water in the low-lying areas. Lloyd did not need to be told that this day would be unlike any he had experienced before.

At about 10:00 a.m., an 8-foot wall of water took the community by surprise. The river went from a width of 225 feet to an estimated 8,500 feet within just a few short hours. The floodwater deafened bystanders, who watched as tons of debris swept past them. Cattle, trees, telephone poles and houses were all pushed relentlessly forward by the wall of water. The *Benkelman Post* described the river's horrific scenery in its special edition on June 7, 1935, as a "vast panorama of dirty yellow water, where thousands of objects were apparent across the expanse of waves."

Accounts in other local newspapers told of residents helplessly watching as people went by on rooftops, screaming for assistance. Their horror increased as they saw the river dash helpless victims against trees or drag them struggling into deep currents, playing with their bodies as they struggled to the surface only to be dragged under again and again. Their mangled bodies reappeared later, shrouded in mud. Bystanders watched as cattle and horses fought to keep their heads above water. Huge one-hundred-year-old trees tumbled downstream. Used by the river as death traps, the trees' roots snagged those struggling to survive and trapped them in a watery grave.

Lloyd and others on the banks cried out in sorrow and helplessness as they recognized friends rushing to certain death on and in floating buildings. The buildings remained intact until they reached a bridge or tree. Hopes were dashed as the river gave no mercy, tearing the structures apart with explosions heard on shore, mingled with the screams of the river's victims dying in the frigid water. The smell of death soon filled the air, a noxious perfume left behind by the manic river. Relief from the disgusting aroma did not arrive until the first hard frost blanketed the ground of the ruined valley in the fall.

Citizens lost in McCook included Glen Bell; Fred McIlvaine; Frances Miller and her children, Charles Francis, Beverly Jean, Virginia and Claudine; Elizabeth Shook; Fred Sullivan; and Fred Swanson.

Located on a hill, McCook escaped most of the flood's fury unscathed. However, the river punished the parts of the community it could reach before racing farther east. Several south-side homes flooded, and the river destroyed the McCook Power Plant, Ravenswood Dairy and Pastime Park. The river halted communication with the outside world, as residents were without electricity for three days. It also fouled the water supply.

Observers recorded two crests, the second higher than the first. Some records show that the Republican rose 10 feet in twelve minutes in McCook,

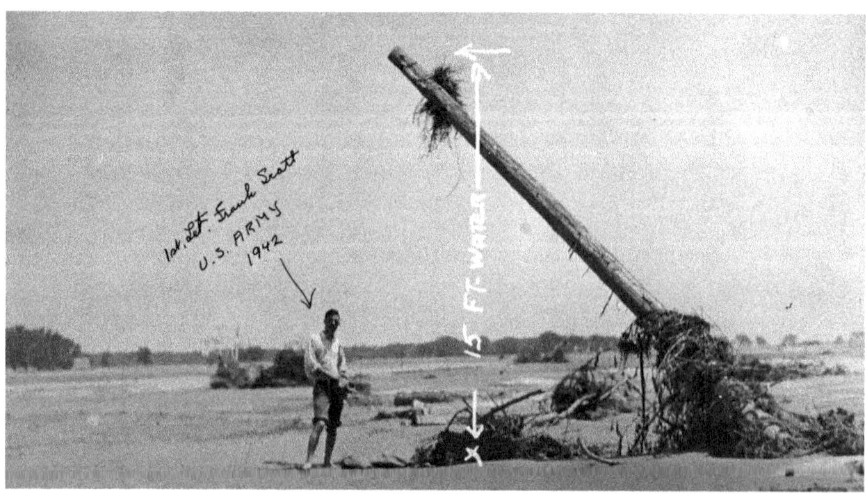

Photo showing the depth of the water at the peak of the flood in McCook. *Museum of the High Plains.*

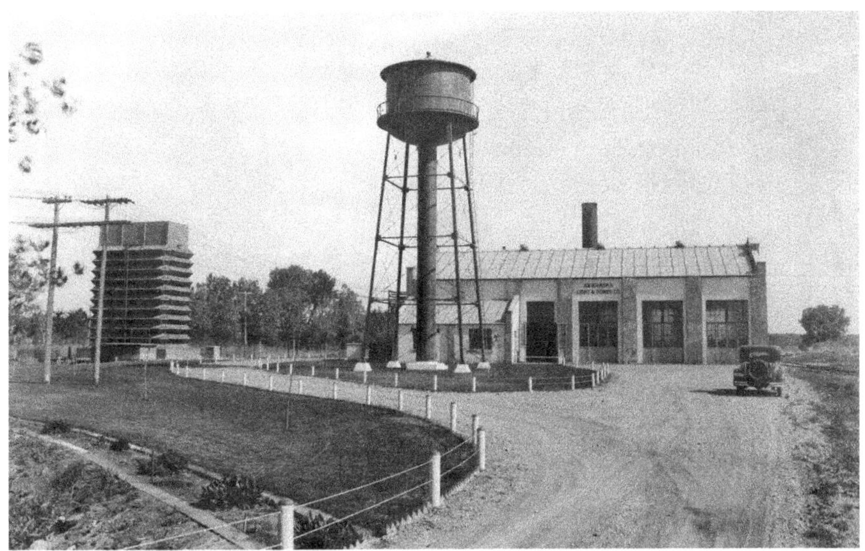

The McCook Power Plant before the flood. *Museum of the High Plains.*

with water 20 feet deep in some places and up to two miles wide. The river grew to an estimated 8,500 feet wide west of McCook, from its normal width of 225 feet, and to 4,100 feet wide east of McCook from 236 feet. One mile west of McCook, the river extended from bluff to bluff for a distance of four miles.

Various people, marooned in McCook when the flood and tornado struck, photographed the drama unfolding before them. They took pictures of the McCook Power Plant, of the standpipe and of bridges and other places as the destruction took place. They witnessed the death of hundreds of helpless cattle and hogs carried away by the swirling water. The animals died as the river dashed them against trees and lashed them with debris.

James Jaquet, general manager of the Nebraska Light and Power Company of McCook, provided a written account of the flood that preserved the tale of heroism and courage exhibited by the workers of the plant and the town's citizens.

The plant, located south of town near present-day Barnett Park, began its life as a flour mill in the early days of settlement in the community. As time passed, workers converted the mill to provide electricity and pump water for the community.

At the time of the flood, the updated structure, a fine, strong building, boasted a steel-framed roof with three sixteen-foot-tall bay doors. The building housed six diesel engines ranging in size from two hundred to nine hundred horsepower, making it one of the largest plants in Nebraska. These engines connected to generators, which produced electricity for the city. Outside the plant, a large water tower held water pumped for city use from wells located across the river. A line extended from the wells to the pump located at the plant.

The men at the plant that morning were familiar with spring flooding on the Republican and took in stride the rising water that had occurred earlier in the month. Each year when the river flooded, workers at the plant filled sandbags to build a wall around the bay doors to prevent water from entering the plant. When the water receded, workers removed the handmade dike and emptied the bags. In the past, their dikes always held, and they removed them when the danger passed. During the slight flooding near the plant a few days before May 31, 1935, a dike of bags had been erected around the plant, and as always, workers emptied them when the danger passed.

At about 4:00 a.m. on the morning of May 31, the operator on duty noticed water beginning to run in the ditch outside the plant. He sent word for additional employees to report to the plant. They began their accustomed task of filling sacks with sand and cinders. A rail car from the Chicago, Burlington and Quincy Railroad, partially full of cinders, the remains of those used a few days earlier to aid in filling the bags, still stood next to the building. Workers already at work quickly put the cinders to use, filling new bags. Additional day workers came to help. By 5:00 a.m., about twelve to fifteen men were working to build a wall of bags around the plant.

The water began to recede, but the men continued to build the wall higher in case the water should rise again. By this time, every regular employee of the plant had reported for work. In addition, word reached town that the plant needed laborers. Several men, in the hope of obtaining a few hours of work, hurried to the plant. Some men completed routine tasks around the plant, while others ran errands to purchase shovels and other needed supplies.

Soon the water began to rise again. Workers filled more bags. Some men went to town to purchase more shovels. The land outside the wall of bags disappeared under water. The men continued to use the cinders from the rail car to fill the bags. The railroad workers brought two more cars of cinders and left them near the plant.

The men felt safe because their new dike was larger and wider than the one torn down previously. They also sandbagged the doors to prevent seepage, just in case some water found its way through the dike. While busy ensuring the safety of the plant, the men failed to notice the access road to the plant

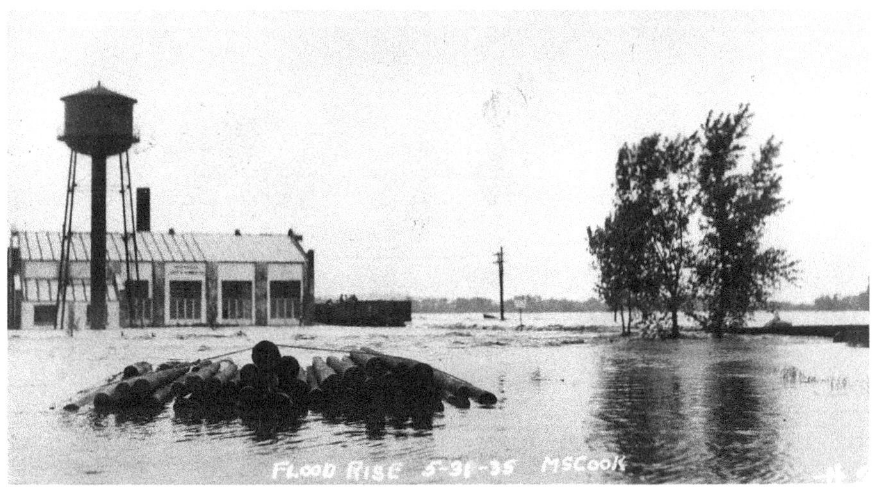

Rising floodwaters threatening the power plant. *Museum of the High Plains.*

slowly being swallowed by the rising river. The devious river trapped them while they worked.

Soon the thirty or more men busy on the dike could not keep up with the water coming over and through the dike. Shouts rang out as the river brushed aside the sandbags at the front of the building. Within seconds, the four-foot wall of bags vanished, and the dike at the rear of the building quickly followed. The river immediately slammed against the large doors of the power plant.

Calls went out to the plant's head office and the dispatcher of the railroad, informing them of the conditions at the plant. A call came in from a McCook businessman urging the men to continue their fight to keep electricity on at all costs during the flood. No one in the plant believed the river could rise much higher until another warning call informed them that in Culbertson, twelve miles west of McCook, the river continued to rise at a rate of two feet every ten minutes.

The men inside the plant, defeated by the rapidly rising water, shut down the large engines at 10:50 a.m. They carefully wrapped the engines to prevent water from entering any critical engine parts, loosened the large engines from their moorings and moved them to what was believed to be a safe location away from the rising water. The staff continued to operate the smaller engines. The river persisted, finally slithering its way into the building. Soon the floor became so wet that continued operation of the small engines endangered the men. At 11:20 a.m., the men shut down the small

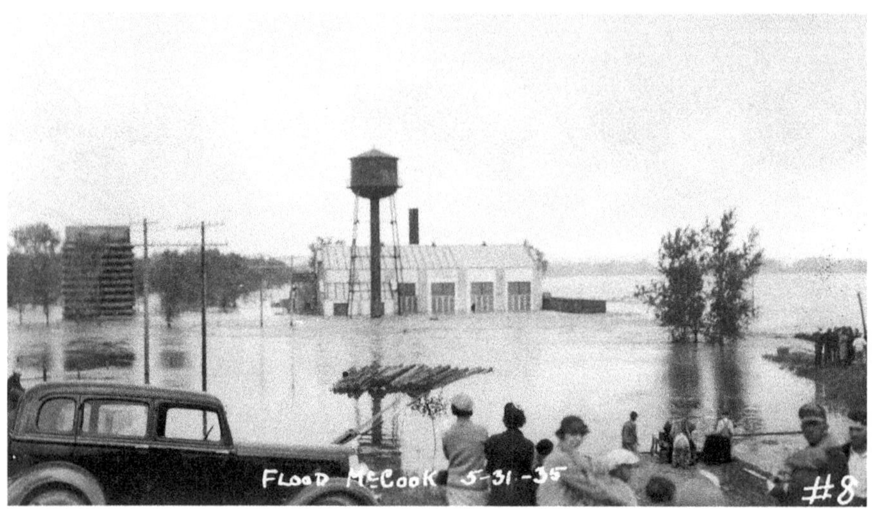

Bystanders watching the power plant. *Museum of the High Plains.*

engines. The motor's generators were dismantled and raised onto the larger engines. Meanwhile, other men bailed water from the plant and the well house, and oil pump pits began to fill with water.

The crash of a collapsing door in the older section of the plant alerted the men of imminent danger. The river, churning round and round the building, finally found a weak spot and wasted no time as it rushed to overcome the structure. The men leapt to safety on top of the engines. One of the men, carrying a length of garden hose, climbed onto a small engine. From his vantage point, he scrambled to the roof through one of the penthouse windows located over the engine.

The men on top of the other engine saw the floodwaters through some of the small windows and wished they could be outside on the rail cars. Those who had been filling bags for the dikes had scrambled onto them as the water rose and now looked safe and comfortable. Then, someone noticed the river moving the heavy cars, and the men gasped as they began to float away. The men on the cars made a mad scramble to reach the west wall of the building. Those inside who could swim dove into the water, which had been rising fast inside the building and was now a frigid five feet deep. They helped the men outside to safety through the lower windows, saving them from being carried away by the river. Two men still outside reached safety by swimming to the building and climbing onto the lower roof of the old part of the plant, aided by the man with the garden hose.

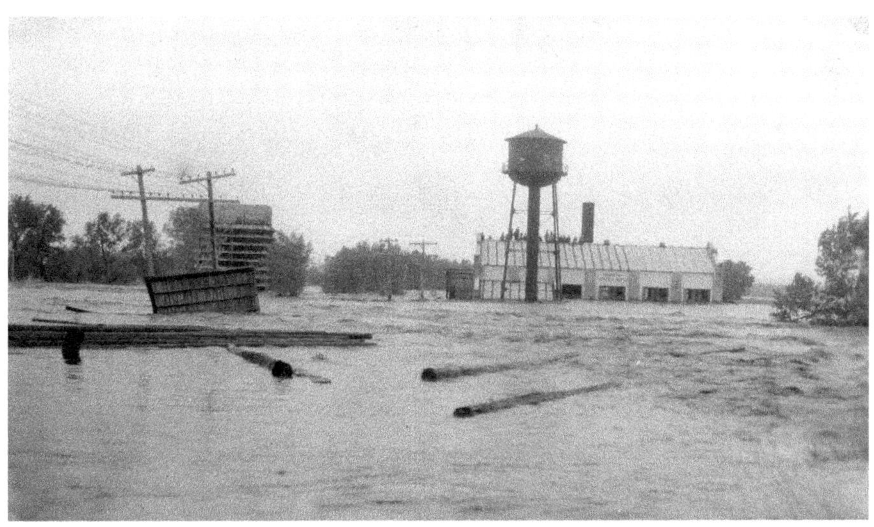

Men watch the floodwaters rise from the roof of the power plant. *Museum of the High Plains.*

The men remaining inside on the large engine realized the rapidly rising river would soon overtake them. Within minutes, they stood in icy water. They tried but failed to make a hole in the roof. Their coworkers already on the roof heard them and began to tear at the roof, attempting to reach them from above. A loud crash, followed by light from an ever-widening hole, rang out as the men on the roof broke through to their friends still trapped below. Unfortunately, one of the men below took a blow to the head from a board used as a battering ram in the rescue. Disregarding his injuries, the injured man worked frantically with the others to enlarge the hole. Soon everyone remaining in the plant scrambled onto the roof with the aid of the men above and the garden hose used as a rescue line.

The men noticed a growing crowd of people on the banks of the river about four hundred feet away. This crowd included their families and friends. However, the roaring river prevented any communication. Even the loudest of voices faded away, drowned out by the thunderous waves. The men felt their chance of escape fading, too.

Some men suggested swimming to shore, but the force of the water soon made it clear they could not survive the attempt. On the bank of the river, it seemed everyone in McCook stood on shore watching the struggle for survival. Those assembled on shore did not stand idle but began immediately to come up with a plan to rescue the stranded men. After much discussion, they agreed to send a rope over to the plant via the electric power poles. A

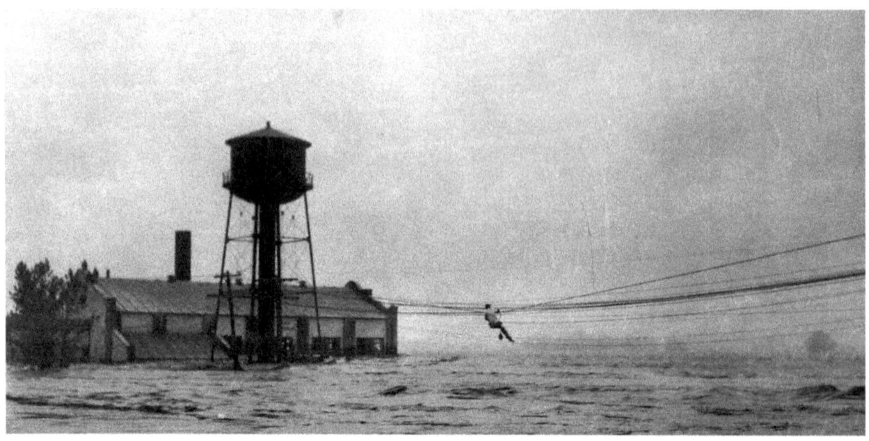

An attempt to rescue men trapped at the McCook Power Plant. *Don Gibson.*

local man, also an expert marksman, used a high-powered rifle to shoot out the insulators on the poles. He took great care, as a missed shot might wound or kill one of the men assembled on the roof. His shots reached their marks. The next step, loosening the wires, allowed a rope to be attached to them. Then, a volunteer, Paul Wilson, pulled himself and the rope across the wires from the shore to the roof of the now otherwise inaccessible building.

A telephone worker's lineman sling, a makeshift breeches buoy, attached to the rope along with a second line, allowed the sling to be pulled back and forth from the roof to land. Crossing the two H-framed poles completed this process. Two men, John Herman and Mike Worske, reached the safety of the shore by this method.

While loading the third man in the sling, the poles gave way, loosened by the power of the floodwaters. Bob French, a twenty-seven-year-old civil engineer at the plant, who had positioned himself on one of the power poles to assist in the rescue, felt the pole break and begin to collapse. As the river tossed him off the pole, he made a perfect dive into the waiting waves below. Amazingly, because of his strong and skillful swimming, he swam with the current and reached a point along the shore. An observer with a horse and buggy kept him in sight and followed his progress in a mad dash along the river's edge. He got as close to French as possible along the shoreline, tossed him a rope and drew him to safety. He finally succeeded in rescuing French by tying the rope around a car body lodged along the shore.

The loss of the power poles and the breeches buoy ended any hope of reaching the remainder of the men on the roof of the power plant. Hopes plummeted further when the water tower also weakened and fell, just missing the roof and the men assembled there. The trapped men felt the building sway as the tank was picked up by the waves and lodged tightly against the building. The crowd on shore froze, listening to the grinding sound coming from the building—the keening death knell of a dying giant. The roof buckled, giving way under the onslaught of debris hurled at it by the malevolent river.

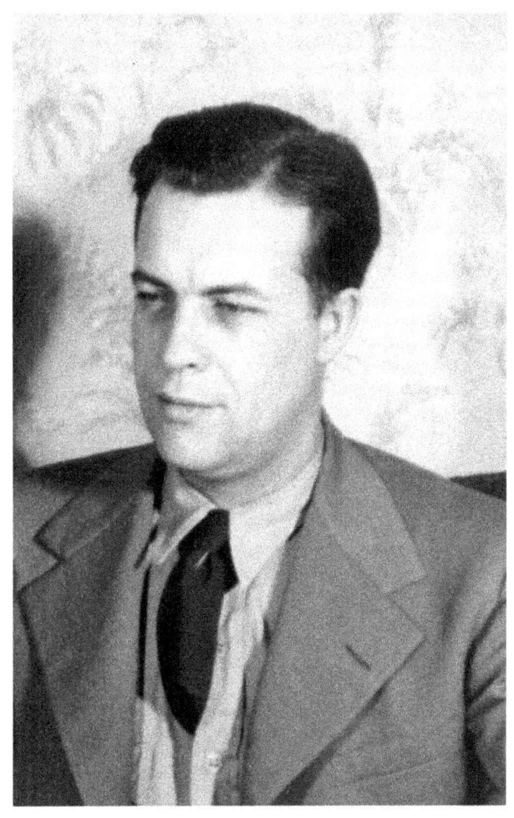

Robert French. *Nancy McKenzie.*

As the day wore on, the men watched as those on shore launched a large pontoon boat. Even with as many as fifty men holding the ropes on the pontoon, the river pulled it out of control, away from shore, and swung it back against the bank. Two other smaller boats, manned by strong young college boys, made similar attempts to reach the men. All of these attempts failed. Nothing proved large enough or powerful enough to reach more than a few feet from shore before being dashed back against the river's banks. The river made repeated attempts to toss the men in the boats overboard, reaching out with angry waves that seemed to roar with fury.

While the crowd tried to come up with another way to rescue the trapped workers, the skies began to darken with ominous clouds on the horizon. In the midst of the desolation, the rain poured down, and the sky turned black. Those with watches lit a match to tell the time: 3:15 p.m. The men on the roof saw a terrible storm building just west of McCook. This storm spawned tornadoes that terrorized the surrounding country and added to the death list.

One tornado went through the Perry, Nebraska area, dense with small farms. It left the ground near Culbertson but dropped again in Frontier

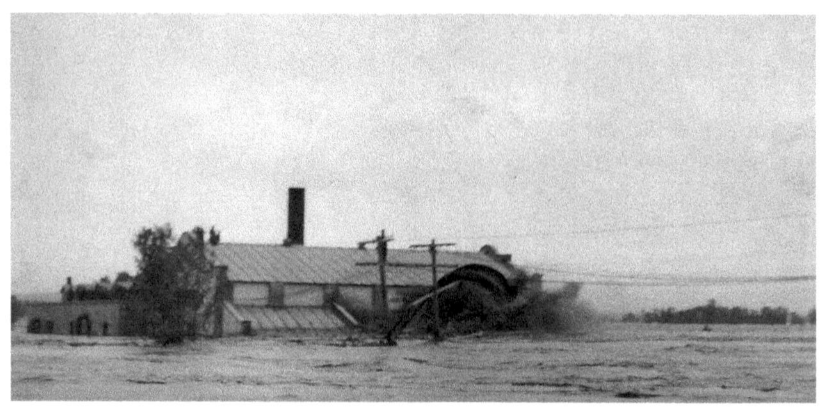

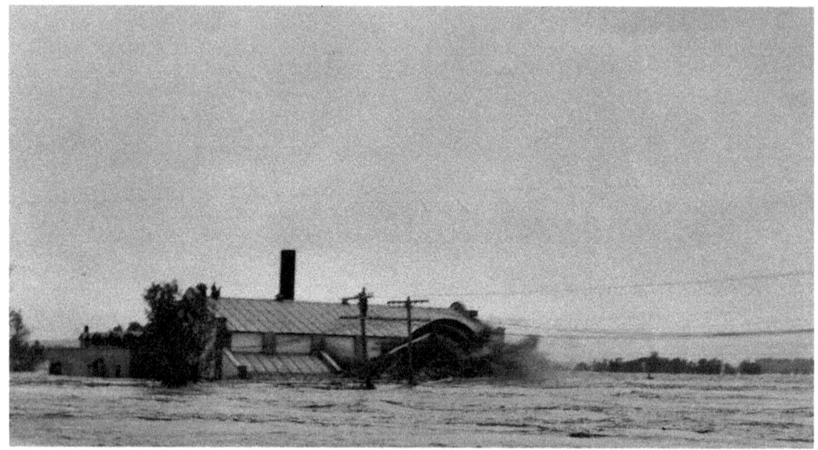

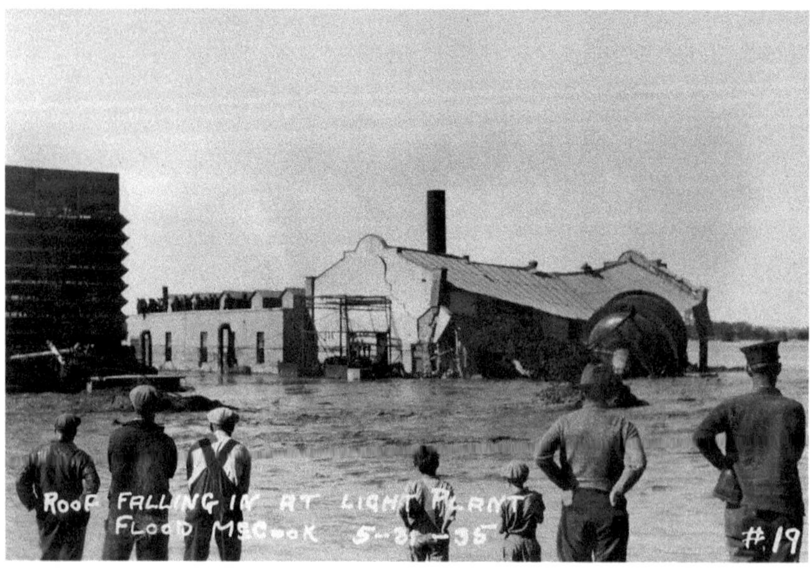
ROOF FALLING IN AT LIGHT PLANT
FLOOD McCOOK
#19

County. Those killed in the Perry area included Anna Zander and her two small sons, Franz Jr. and Gerhardt, caught outside on their way to the storm cellar. Two other children also lost their lives: a one-week-old baby, Ruth, daughter of Mr. and Mrs. Ross Stratton, and Pauline Rhodes, two-year-old daughter of Mr. and Mrs. William Rhodes. Fourteen families reported damage ranging from having their roofs torn off to complete destruction, with their farmsteads wiped clean of house, barn and outbuildings. At one home sixteen miles south of Curtis, Nebraska, the only trace left of the farmstead's existence was the empty sidewalks. The storm continued, traveling north and east and damaging forty-two homes and 144 buildings. It injured thirty-five people, some so severely that they died a few days later.

Telephone lines snapped. Hail did extensive damage to buildings and the already stressed crops in the surrounding fields. But in McCook, hardly anyone noticed the western sky as they watched the men on the power plant roof. The rain had stopped, and newly developed towering red clouds caught the crowd's attention as they passed overhead. A dust storm thick with powdery red soil—typical of storms coming from the south, laden with Oklahoma dust—blew for thirty minutes, leaving the men, previously soaked to the skin by rain and floodwater, now covered in dirt.

As twilight fell, the men at the plant plunged into despair. They could feel the building sway as the floodwaters raged past their perch on the damaged building. The water did not rise further, but the force did not lessen as the night wore on. The men felt the walls supporting the damaged roof begin to weaken. They dreaded their fall into the inky darkness, should the roof collapse. They mentally calculated their chance of survival in the terrible waves of the still-roaring river.

Cheers rang out from the roof when those on shore began bringing their cars and trucks to the riverbank. Family and friends turned their vehicle lights on the plant and illuminated the men huddled there. Without waiting to be told, the Burlington Railroad men brought their engine around. They directed its light on the men. It revealed pale, anxious faces peering out over the roaring water until a heavy rain at midnight forced most of those keeping watch on shore to take shelter.

Opposite, top: The power plant's water tower collapsing. *Museum of the High Plains.*

Opposite, middle: The water tank after collapsing. *Nancy McKenzie.*

Opposite, bottom: The roof of the power plant collapses. *Museum of the High Plains.*

The lights provided the only comfort the marooned men received that night. Soaked to the skin by the floodwaters, drenched again by the heavy rain and then coated in dirt, they found no protection from the incessant wind, which chilled them to the bone. Some of the men slept lying together in a large group. Periodically, those on the outside, the coldest area, moved to the inside of the group so no one suffered in the biting wind too long. Some men, unable to sleep, paced the roof, keeping watch through the night. Uncomfortable and hungry, not one of the men visibly panicked or complained.

The men welcomed the dawn, as the sunshine provided cheer and warmth. They spent the morning watching as those on shore made several more attempts to reach them. One man looked toward shore in the strengthening light. He was cheered to see his waiting wife waving to him. Another woman could be heard crying, "My God, why don't they do something?" The other observers on shore, as well as the men at the plant, soon realized nothing could be done until the river yielded and released the men from their prison.

Finally, as morning turned to afternoon, the water began to subside. A small boat manned by Max Merrill, a skilled boatman who spent his boyhood on the Mississippi, reached the roof, bringing coffee, water and sandwiches. The men rejoiced in their first meal in over twenty-four hours.

Another boat followed, and rescuers took the men two or three at a time to the safety of the shoreline. No one rushed to be rescued. The manager of the plant, James Jaquet, found it necessary to call out the names of the men he believed should be taken to shore first. Later still, the remaining men waded to a sandbar created near the plant's cooling tower. From there, a larger boat took seven or eight men at a time to shore.

By 2:30 p.m. on June 1, the last man had reached shore. While all suffered from exposure, hunger and dehydration, no one sustained serious injuries. When cleanup efforts began, the men realized that the river, in its fury to destroy the building, had made two serious mistakes. The cinder cars that floated behind the building diverted much of the heaviest current from the wall supporting the rear section of the roof, which kept it from collapsing. The water tower had collapsed at the front of the building; however, it did not bring the building down and instead acted as a trap for a large portion of the debris thrown against the fragile walls. This kept the front portion of the roof from totally collapsing under the weight of the mounting pile of trash, debris and dead animals that collected in and around the tower.

Workers assisting in the cleanup discovered the building packed with mud, trees, branches, leaves and the bodies of cows, coyotes and other small

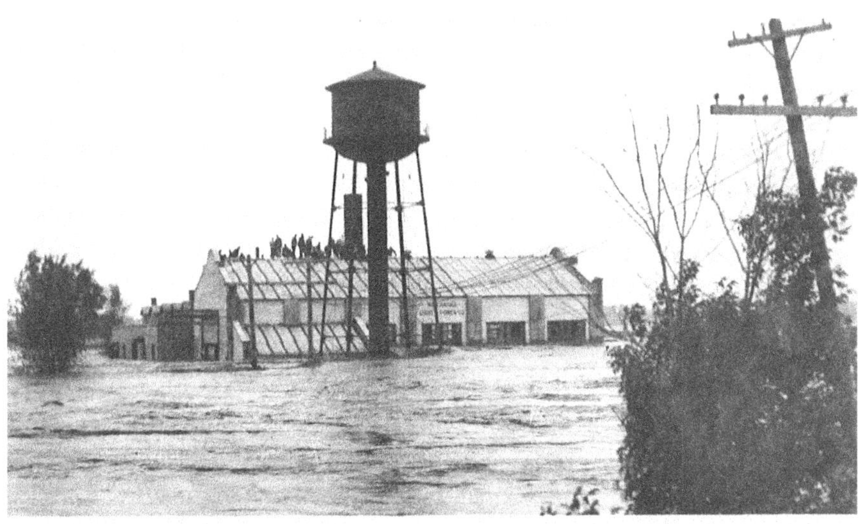

Jake Amen	C. H. England	Hugh Meyers
Floyd Albright	W. R. Evans	E. J. Nelson
F. W. Anthony	R. H. French	W. Rishel
W. Baker	Frank Gillen	C. C. Parker
John Baker	John Herbst	Geo. Schleeman
Cloyd Bell	John Herman	Geo. Simmons
T. C. Bergin	Merl Huet	J. L. Snyder
Floyd Bower	A. S. Hockman	Ed. Sterr
Chas. Clark	J. R. Jaquet	Gunnar Swanson
Oscar Clark	Harry Jensen	Stewart Walker
Carl Cottingham	Ray Lytle	Paul Wilson
Lou Dulaney	V. Lytle	Louis Wolfe
Ralph Elwood	Elmer Mapes	Mike Worski
		Joe Ward

A list of men trapped in the power plant taken from Jaquet's report. *Museum of the High Plains.*

animals. Snakes trapped in the remnants of the building made cleanup especially dangerous. Amazingly, the workmen retrieved the engines, wrapped so carefully before the river took over the building, and quickly put them back into service after dismantling and cleaning them thoroughly. For the next several days, two hundred men worked steadily cleaning out the building. They moved the old equipment to higher ground and within two weeks had restored service to the McCook community.

Carol Wolf related how proud her grandfather Louis felt about his role in the work at the plant before, during and after the flood. He took great pride in restoring power to the community so quickly. He told his children stories about his harrowing night on the roof. Carol's mother told them how she

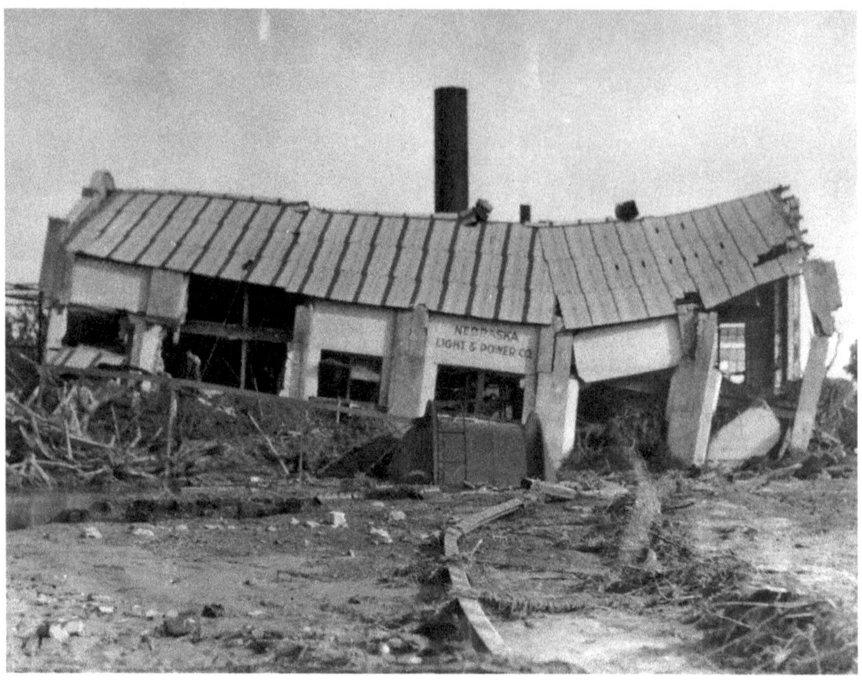

The destroyed power plant. *Museum of the High Plains.*

waited on shore and worried about Louis, her fiancé, trapped in the violent waters of the Republican.

Because McCook is located on a hill, only seven houses partially flooded. Five washed away from their original location, and two moved partially off their foundations. One lodged in the bridge near the power plant, and the river destroyed it completely. Later, workers moved the remaining houses to new foundations on higher ground.

While the men at the power plant struggled to survive, other residents, like Lloyd Harvey, worried about their relatives downriver. Marlene Harvey Wilmot recorded Lloyd's entire adventure in her book *Bluff to Bluff*. Following is a portion of that story.

Lloyd's mother and father-in-law, Frank and Anna Voight, lived in Republican City, about seventy miles downstream. They lived very close to the riverbank. He knew that if they did not get out of the valley, they would have no chance of survival. Lloyd tried for hours to get in touch with his wife's parents by telephone. Finally, by having the telephone company route a call north through North Platte and east to Omaha, he was able to reach them. His father-in-law started to tell Lloyd how many floods they had

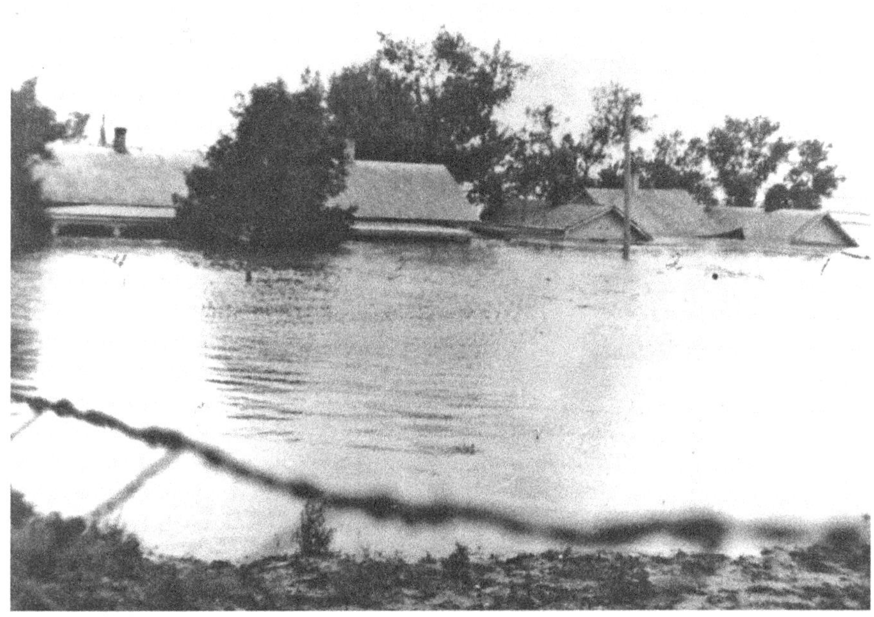

Flooded homes south of McCook, Nebraska. *Museum of the High Plains.*

survived with no difficulty. Lloyd simply said this flood was different than any ever seen in the valley before. He told Frank he should take his family and get out of the valley immediately.

After he telephoned his in-laws, Lloyd's wife, Freda, was still worried that her parents would never leave the valley. Lloyd worried, too, so he stopped by his office to tell his supervisor he was going to try to get to his in-laws' home. A boy named Eddie Kotinick was at the office and asked if he could ride along. They started from the Fruit Company not knowing how far they would be able to go. After driving about six miles east of McCook, they found that the highway bridge crossing Red Willow Creek had washed out. There was no use turning north, as they knew all the bridges in that direction would be washed out, too.

Luckily, Lloyd knew the area well. He struck out south, where he knew a small wooden bridge crossed Willow Creek about half a mile below the highway bridge. He found it covered with eighteen inches of water. Lloyd got out of the car, took off his shoes and socks and waded into the water to check the condition of the road and the safety of the bridge. He observed that the bridge's guardrails were missing but that the road still felt firm, and the bridge planks seemed solid. He returned to the car and drove slowly across the bridge toward Indianola.

East of Indianola, dead animals on the highway were piled so high it was nearly impossible to find a path wide enough to go around them. Lloyd and Eddie discovered that the highway bridges were also washed out, so they again left the main highway. Following an adjacent, older road along the north bluff, they reached Cambridge. Again, they found highway and railroad bridges washed out.

They stopped to visit with a group of people beside parked cars on the east side of Medicine Creek. Like the Red Willow, bridges along the Medicine had vanished, leaving those assembled with no way to proceed. Nearby, the railroad crossing had also washed away, leaving only the rails of the crossing intact, precariously suspended just above the water and weighted down by a few wooden ties stubbornly clinging to them. Lloyd called out to the people on the east side of the creek. He asked if they had tried to cross over the rails. Someone called back, telling him they all feared falling into the thundering river below. Lloyd walked over to the rails and stepped up on them. After jumping up and down a few times to test the strength of the metal, he determined they could hold his weight. He crawled across the rails over the rising water. When he looked back after reaching the other side, he was surprised to see Eddie right behind him.

The waiting crowd on the east included two men from McCook, both frantic to get home to check on their families. Both of these men worked for an auto parts dealer and arrived at the washed-out creek in a light-panel company truck. Lloyd struck a deal with the men. He would take their truck to check on his in-laws while they took his car to go home to McCook to check on their families. They promised to return to pick up Lloyd and Eddie at 8:00 p.m. the same evening so that they could all return to their homes in McCook. Lloyd gave the men instructions on how to avoid the washed-out bridges on their trip home. He and Eddie then struck out east again. When they reached their destination, they discovered the Voight family waiting in a vacant house in Republican City. The home was located above the river bridge a short distance from their former river bottom home. While Lloyd and Eddie made the trip, the Voights heeded Lloyd's warnings. They worked through the night using a wagon and team of horses to bring canned food and farm animals from their farm in the valley to higher ground. In the early morning hours, Frank decided to walk back and return with the family car. As he approached the river bridge, he looked upstream and saw a wall of water rapidly approaching. He immediately turned and hurried back the way he had come. He missed being trapped on the valley side of the bridge by only minutes.

Lloyd's brother, Leslie Harvey, was working on the south side of the river at the time. He witnessed the wall of water as it hit the Voight home. He reported that the force of the water was so strong that the barn and the farmhouse exploded, sweeping the resulting debris away. The Voights lost their home, all of their personal belongings and the family car. Later, their heavy iron cookstove was found a quarter mile away from where the house once stood. They found their destroyed car several miles downriver but never recovered any of their other possessions.

After determining the Voight family was safe, Eddie and Lloyd drove into Holdrege to send a report of the disaster to Lloyd's company office in Hastings. They then headed back to retrieve Lloyd's car and return to McCook. Heavy rain slowed their trip. Although Eddie and Lloyd returned later than they agreed, arriving at 8:30 p.m., the McCook men had waited for them, afraid to return by themselves to McCook in the downpour. Lloyd, confident he could get back safely, drove home. It took three and a half hours to make the twenty-six-mile trip. They pulled into McCook at midnight, driving in heavy rain the entire trip.

Cleanup and rescue efforts near McCook began as quickly as people could navigate the floodwaters. Sadly, this meant many horrific discoveries for those determined to help their neighbors. The body of Elizabeth Shook, flood victim from the Miller home near McCook, was found with her purse still hooked over her arm. According to Wilmot, workers found her eighteen miles east of McCook and positively identified her by her school paycheck, still tucked inside her purse.

Many other victims remain unidentified, including a small girl, possibly four years old, whose only identifying feature was her white shoes. Four American Legion planes brought in from Grand Island searched for victims. Powerboats brought upriver to McCook from Omaha searched every stream and channel first for the living and, later, for the dead.

Chapter 9

On Through Nebraska

Indianola

On the morning of May 31, 1935, Lottie Guthrie started her baking as usual, placing her wedding ring on the windowsill for safekeeping. She and her husband, Lee, lived south of Indianola on the river bottom with their eight children. When news of the approaching flood reached their home, the entire family (with the exception of their eldest, Carl, who was working away from home) rushed into a farm wagon pulled by a team of horses. Taken by surprise, Lottie joined the family, leaving her baking unfinished and her wedding ring on the sill. They drove to Indianola, never to see their home again. Their house, and Lottie's wedding ring, disappeared in the floodwaters soon after they drove away. Like so many, assured of the safety of his own family, Lee quickly returned to the river to help other families get to higher ground. He participated in several daring rescues.

Cambridge

On the evening of the flood, Geoffrey King, an employee of the Nebraska Highway Department, took a ride with his fiancée in her new car. They traveled between Holbrook and Cambridge on a newly built and freshly graveled state highway. When they noticed water approaching the edges of

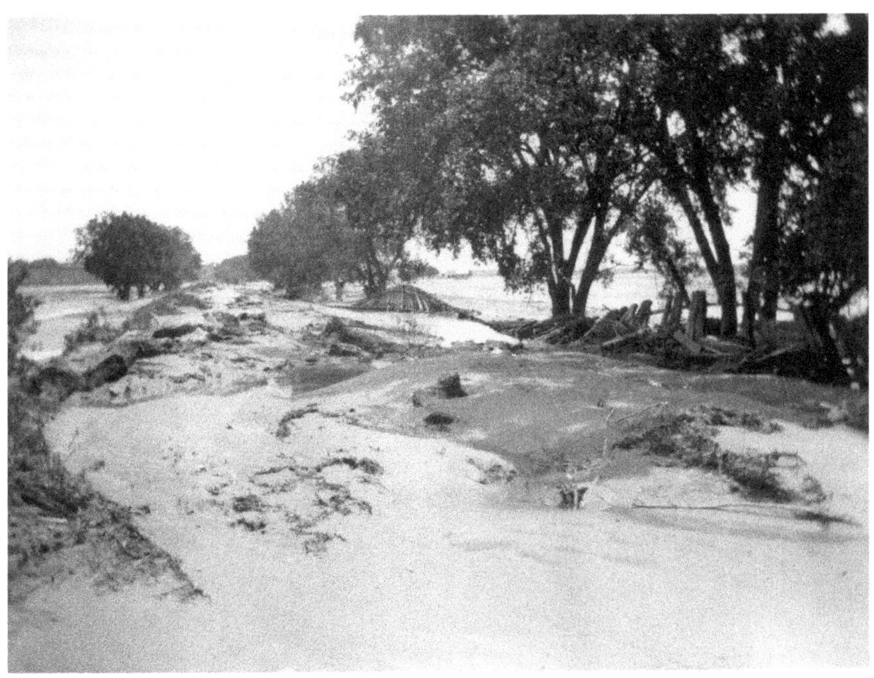

Destruction and debris left in the wake of the floodwaters. *Joseph Torrey.*

the highway, they returned to Holbrook. By the time darkness fell that night, Cambridge had flooded. The new highway had disappeared, along with the railroad tracks running beside it.

Bob Stewart, twelve years old and living in Indianola at the time, decided he would like to see a flood. Along with some friends, he walked to Cambridge to watch the river rise. The boys arrived about the time most folks in town were eating supper and just about the time the wall of water hit. Bob and his friends, safe on a high bank, watched in horror as homes washed by. As the houses crumpled, they saw occupants sucked from inside the wreckage. Gasping and fighting the dangerous debris, these unwary victims quickly vanished, pulled beneath the roaring waves. The river also trapped Bob and his friends. Cut off from Indianola completely, three days went by before Bob and his friends found a way to let their families know they were safe.

Losses of life in Cambridge included three-year-old Kenneth Moseley, George Sayer and, in one of the strangest stories to come from Cambridge during the flood, the death of the Reverend T.M. Bragg.

Reverend Bragg and his invalid wife, Nettie, were trapped in their home in the south part of Cambridge during the flood. The two were huddled together in their home when the floodwaters picked it up from its foundation. The house started to move until stopped by some nearby trees. The shocked Braggs stood together in the center of their parlor when water and mud suddenly came pouring in through the doors and windows. Water quickly rose to Reverend Bragg's waist. Abruptly, he said, "I think we have to go!" and fell into the water, dead of an apparent heart attack.

Nettie remained in the home, calling for her husband while debris began to accumulate around her feet. She would trample it down and then step up on the resulting mound rising higher and higher. Eventually, she stood on such a large mass that her head tilted against the ceiling. She felt the river surrounding her legs and body with debris and mud. Her long hair loosened and tangled in the debris.

Neighbors discovered her the next morning at about 11:00 a.m. Rescuers feared that some in their group would be killed in the treacherous waters still swirling in the house. Before they were able to cut Nettie free from the deadly trap, twenty-five men would be needed to rescue her, as the still-dangerous river seemed reluctant to give up its tightly bound victim. Determined to live for the sake of her daughter, she refused to give up hope throughout the ordeal. Nettie also insisted that her husband lay just below her in the debris, but searches of the house and the surrounding area were unsuccessful.

Other Cambridge residents faced similar challenges. According to the June 6, 1935 issue of the *Cambridge Clarion*, when the flood entered their home, Henry Kehr, age sixty-five and afflicted with rheumatism so severe he

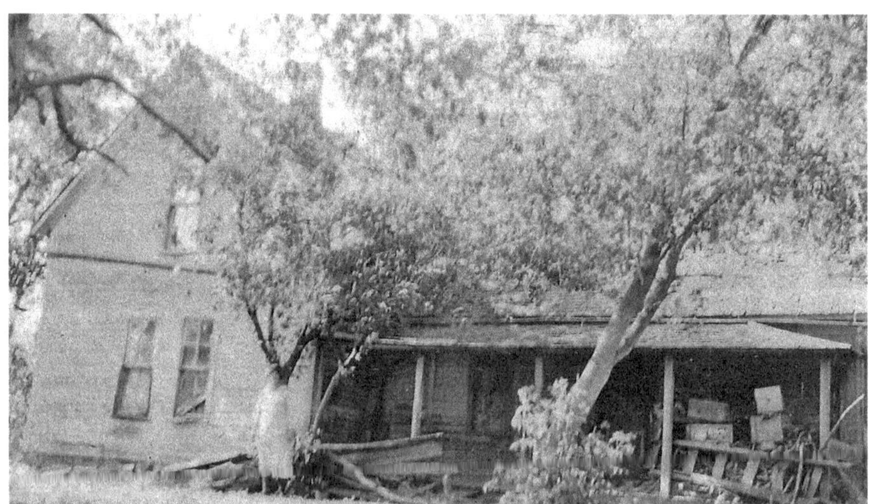

Reverend Bragg's home after the floodwaters had receded. *Cambridge Museum.*

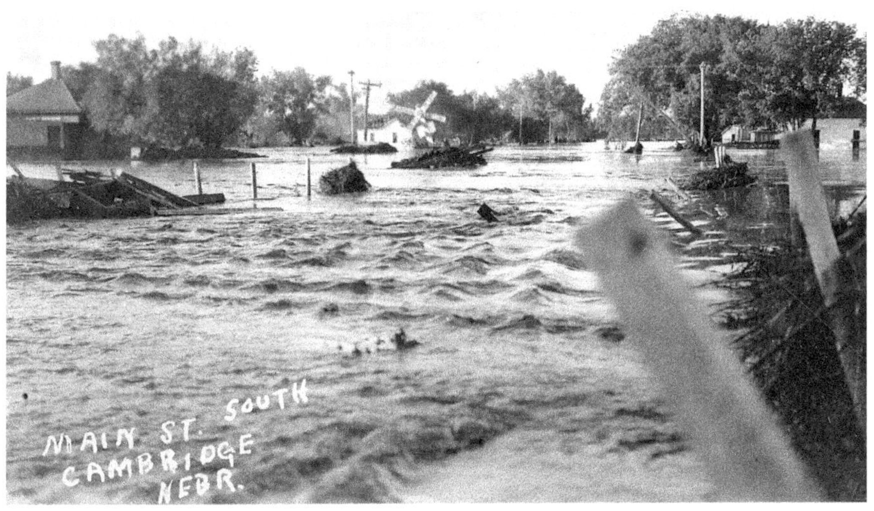

South Main Street after the flood. Note the eleven people trapped on the roof of the house in the distance past the railroad crossing sign. *Cambridge Museum.*

had to walk with a cane, pushed his 275-pound wife into the attic through a hole in the ceiling measuring three feet by eighteen inches. Henry had not worked in years, having lost his strength. However, the terror of the flood renewed his vigor, much to the surprise of both Henry and his wife.

Mrs. Russell Henry stated that when she saw the flood coming, she opened all the doors and windows in the house. Then she put her five children on the roof and joined them, bringing along the supper that had been cooking on the stove.

The Messersmith family, who lived thirty miles northeast of Cambridge in Frontier County, went to look at the floodwaters at Medicine Creek and then traveled on to Cambridge. On the way home, it became as dark as night with rain so heavy they could not see the road. The family stopped at the Orofino Post Office and learned that their farm had been destroyed by a tornado while they were away.

ARAPAHOE

The flood, especially severe at Arapahoe, took seven lives before the ordeal ended. The victims included Will Andrews and his wife, Dessie; George Hayes; Ray, Joe and Edward Kirwin; and John Misterek.

Men working at the flour mill south of Arapahoe on May 31 heeded warnings about the approaching flood and stayed to keep the basement of the mill pumped out. They were trapped there without food or water for forty-eight hours. Arapahoe remained cut off for some time as creeks overflowed on all sides of the community.

EDISON

High water created havoc in Edison as well. Over eight inches of water entered the post office, and all other businesses had equally high floodwaters with which to contend. Every basement in town filled with water, and buildings in low-lying areas vanished. The river cut a new channel about a half mile north of its old pathway.

Bill Manley reported that he and his father went to warn a neighbor located about a mile west of Edison about the flood. The neighbor and three friends, playing cards when they arrived, were unconcerned. They merely picked up the card table and moved upstairs while Bill and his father went on to warn others. Later, Bill learned that mud, deposited up to the ceiling of the first floor below, had trapped the card players in the second story for quite some time. When the water went down, the high-water mark in the house reached the thirteenth stair of the home.

Bill and his family spent over two months helping other neighbors clean up after the flood. During that time, they were unlucky enough to find the body of an elderly woman. However, due to the poor condition of her body caused by the buzzards that had called attention to her location, she remains unidentified.

The old river bridge in Edison stood high and dry while the river flowed in a new channel about a half mile north of its original location. Over three hundred people spent the night in Edison on Cemetery Hill after the town flooded. When the local druggist realized the electricity would not be restored quickly, the children in town were delighted when he passed out free ice cream cones. These were the last served for almost a month until the store's refrigeration could be restored.

OXFORD

Laura Swindell Cowan described the emotional state of many in the Oxford area after the flood: "We were all numb, and wanted to be around others; no one wanted to be alone!" The shock of the many still missing hung over the town like a black cloud of despair.

The National Guard in Nebraska was deployed to help in the disaster. Units came from Hastings, Kearney, Lexington and Holdrege. Some of the younger guards, like Roy Pearson of Holdrege, age sixteen, had no experience with or training for such a disaster. Nevertheless, they quickly became involved in rescuing those trapped in the floodwaters, particularly important in the Oxford area.

The heaviest loss of life from the flood occurred in the Oxford area, with over one-fourth of the deaths taking place in this area. When the rescues turned to the recovery of bodies, the Guardsmen were assigned these duties as well. They were also instrumental in helping to clean up the massive amount of destruction left in the flood's wake.

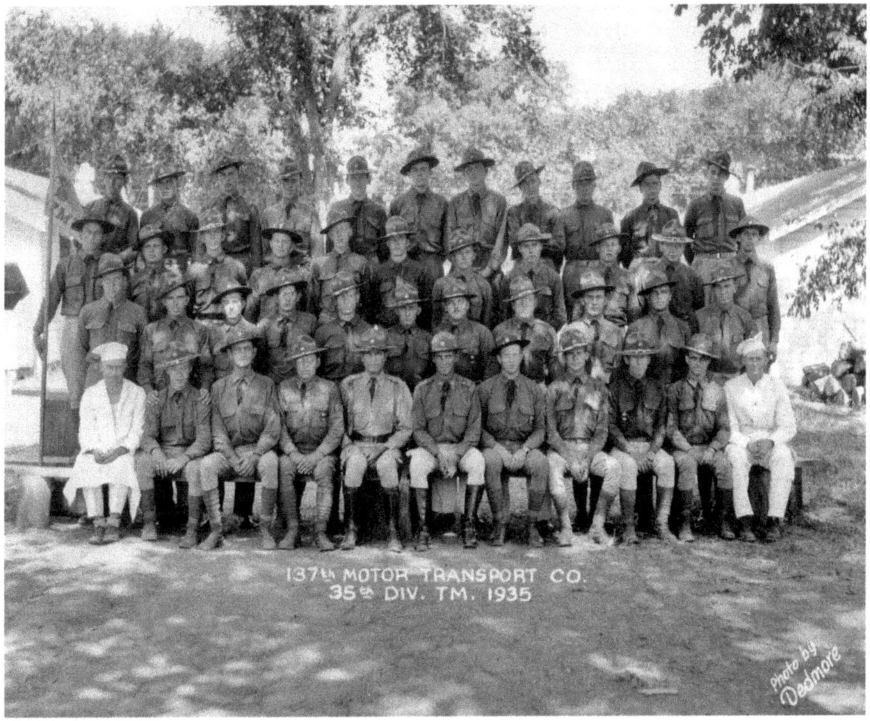

Nebraska National Guardsmen who assisted in flood recovery efforts. *Roy Pearson.*

One of the greatest tragedies in the Oxford area involved the Fuchs family. Charles and Martha Fuchs lived on a farm near Oxford. Their son Orville lived across the road from them. Orville's family included his wife, Dorothy, and their two children, Howard and Willis Lou. Nearby, Orville's brother Herman lived with his wife, Mary, and his wife's daughter, Virginia Blauvelt. Also in Herman's home that day were other family members: Mary's brother, Ralph Blauvelt, and Leona and Carl Anderson.

When the flood struck, everyone happened to be at Orville's house. They all went to the attic when the water started pouring in the house. Orville chopped a hole in the ceiling so the family could get out onto the roof. Charles went first, followed by the rest of the family. Just after they got outside onto the roof, the house came loose from its foundation and quickly began moving down the river. Herman and Charles fell into the water but managed to find safety in some nearby trees. Meanwhile, the house struck a tree and broke in two, throwing the remaining family members into the water.

Orville saw his daughter vanish beneath the floodwaters. His mother and other family members were also swept downstream. Deeply distressed, he vowed to save the rest of his family. Orville tried to swim to safety while carrying his son and with Dorothy clinging to his overalls. He was very strong and an excellent swimmer, but he could not save his wife. After losing her grip on his clothing and being struck savagely by debris, the river dragged Dorothy away downstream. Debris also struck Orville with a blow to the back of his head so severe that it broke out one of his teeth. Undaunted, he clung tenaciously to his son and continued to make his way toward shore.

Orville swam to a small island, where he and his son Howard were joined by the family dog, Jack. Thirty-six hours passed before rescuers arrived. National Guard members who managed to get a boat to the trio's precarious location protested when Orville picked up the dog. No animals were allowed on board any rescue craft. Orville vowed he would remain on the island if they did not help his dog. Finally, they agreed to take the animal.

Once the boat reached land, Jack jumped off as soon as his family reached the safety of the shore. Orville and Howard were united with Charles and Herman in a temporary shelter established at Gupton's Garage. Jack was last seen running back to where the Fuchs home once stood. Orville and his family found the dog waiting when they returned to the farm.

The list of dead in the area included Leona Anderson and her son Carl; Glen Anderson; John DeVries and his wife, Rena, as well as Rena's son Chester Schultz, who had just graduated from high school; the Fuchs family, including Martha, Willis Lou, Dorothy, Mary, Virginia and Ralph

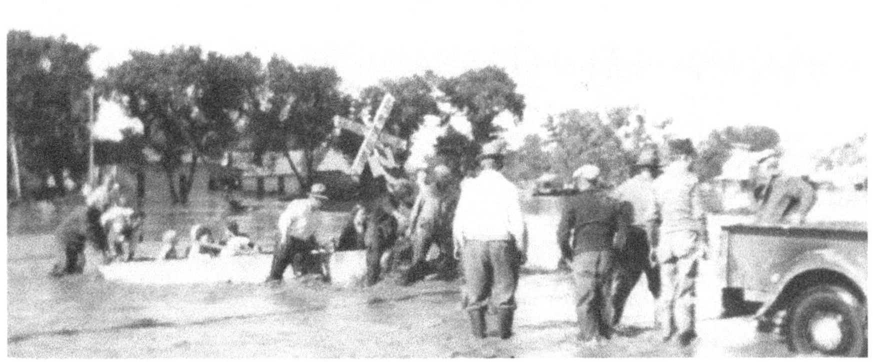

Rescue workers bringing in survivors. *Cambridge Museum.*

Blauvelt; Mart Madison; James and Emma Mills; and Fred Nordstrom. The recovery of all their bodies proved to be especially difficult. The deaths were also especially disturbing because warnings had come in as early as 5:00 a.m. on the morning of the flood. Unfortunately, many failed to heed the warnings and decided to stay in the bottomland. When the flood struck, houses toppled like toys, and those trapped inside were thrown about like dolls. Whole families were swept downriver. Few who remained in the river bottom after the warnings came survived.

ORLEANS

Because the flood came rushing into Orleans at night, and because people did not believe the flood could possibly be as bad as the rumors circulated prior to the flood, Orleans suffered great losses, and many perished. Repeated line rings from telephone operators went unheeded, and many along the river bottom who did not have telephones had no warning at all.

Losing their lives in the community and the surrounding area were Earl Anderson; Ray Bickford; Minnie Dake; Francis Delmont; William and Carrie Lacy; Mart Madison; Martran Modsos; Henry and Irene Neumeyer and their children, Dorothy and George; Elvira, Lester and Anna Schachtler; and William Stevens and his wife, Emma, along with William's mother, Mary, and their two grandchildren, Billie Pat and Jacqueline.

ALMA

In a sad repetition of the experience of their neighbors upriver, many in the Alma area refused to believe that the river could flood their homes, and many died. Arlene Dake, who lived near Alma, survived despite having no warning. The flood reached her home at night, roaring in like a freight train. Soon water poured in all the windows of her home. Within minutes, the walls began to crack as if they were made of eggshells. The river rushed in and carried Arlene away. Fighting to keep her head above water, she grabbed a grapevine hanging from a tree and pulled herself to safety. She would spend the next thirty-two hours there, finally rescued by her brothers, who had set out in a boat to search for their missing family members.

Arlene suffered severe health problems as a result of the flood. The nerves in her legs were permanently damaged from her hours spent crouched in the tree. She endured blood poisoning in both legs and struggled with pneumonia. When asked about the key to her survival, she stated that she had made up her mind not to panic and felt no fear during her ordeal; she

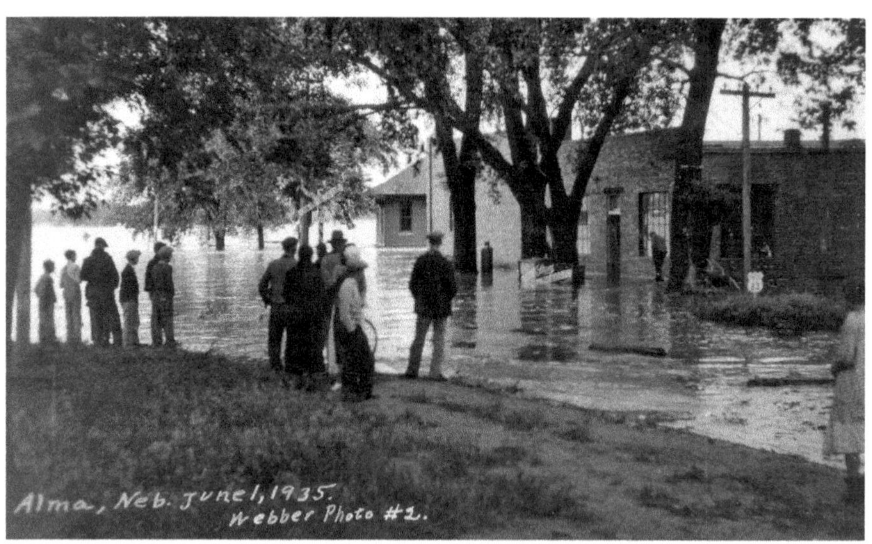

Highway 83, Alma, Nebraska. *Joseph Torrey.*

Opposite, top: Alma Depot, June 1, 1935. *Joseph Torrey.*

Opposite, middle: Sunlight Produce Company, Alma, June 1, 1935. *Joseph Torrey.*

Opposite, bottom: The Ekberg farm near Alma, Nebraska. *Joseph Torrey.*

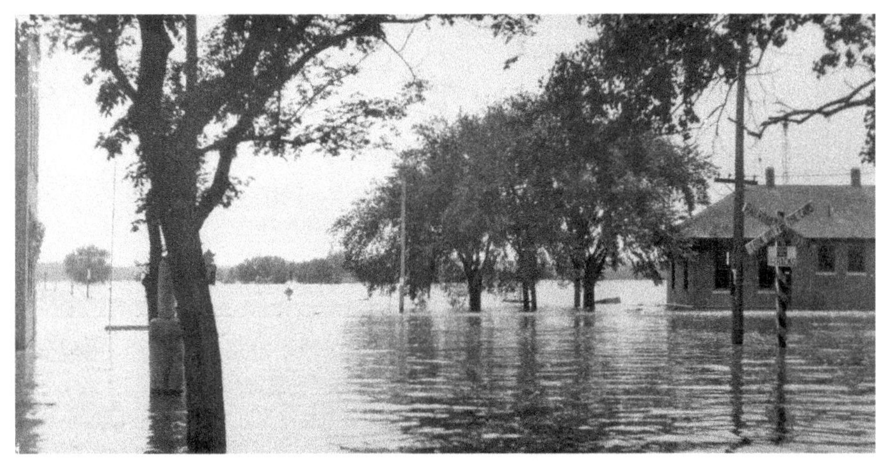

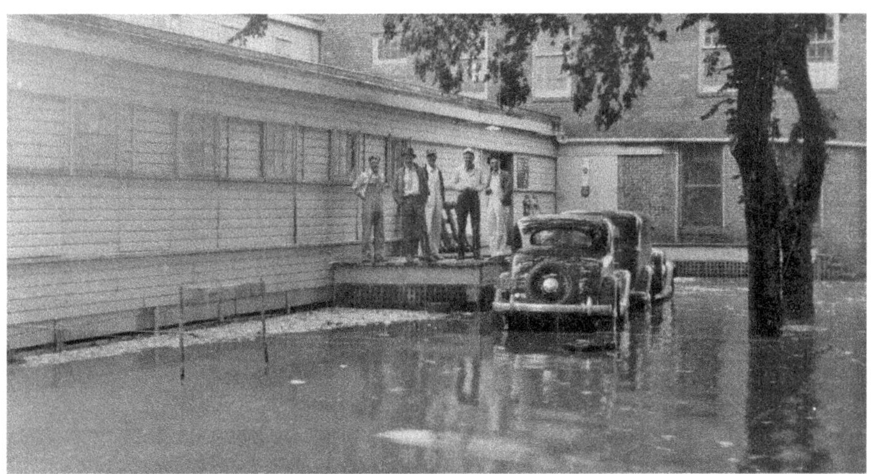

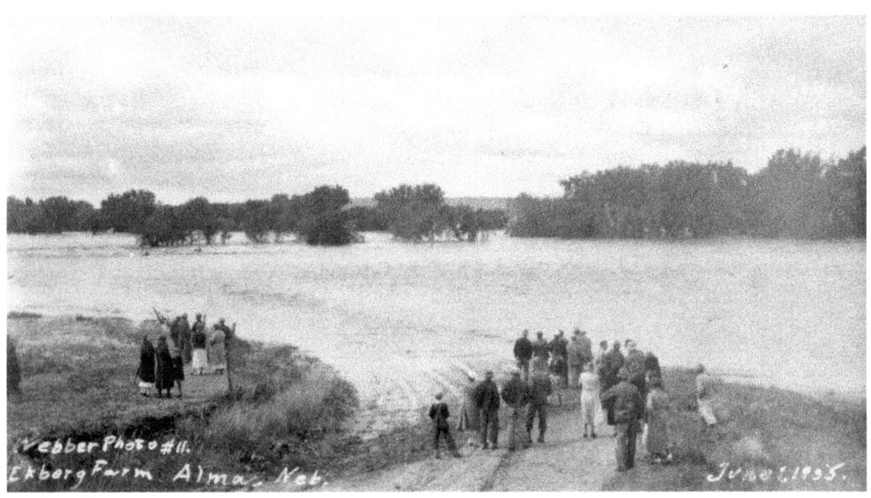
Photo #11.
Ekberg Farm Alma, Neb.
June 1935.

was confident she would be rescued. This helped her to survive while in the water and helped her endure her long and painful ordeal while waiting in the tree for rescue.

Naponee

Happily, those who heard the midnight warning of the coming flood near Naponee heeded it. Only one person needed rescue, although the community suffered high property loss. Bernice Haskins Post wrote in her memoirs that "the sight was such a shock." She remembered watching with her family as the flood came down the river. At first, the river remained in its banks and looked normal—except for the fact that it moved as a solid mass of debris, so thick that it looked like you could walk across its surface. Behind the mat of trash came a wall of water four feet high, filling the river bottom from bluff to bluff. Bernice's family watched in horror as it twisted off the rails on the railroad tracks as if they were paper, sweeping them along down the river.

Clifford Rebman, the night telephone operator in Naponee at the time of the flood, took the warnings for his community seriously. The telephone operator in Oxford called Clifford at two minutes to twelve and warned

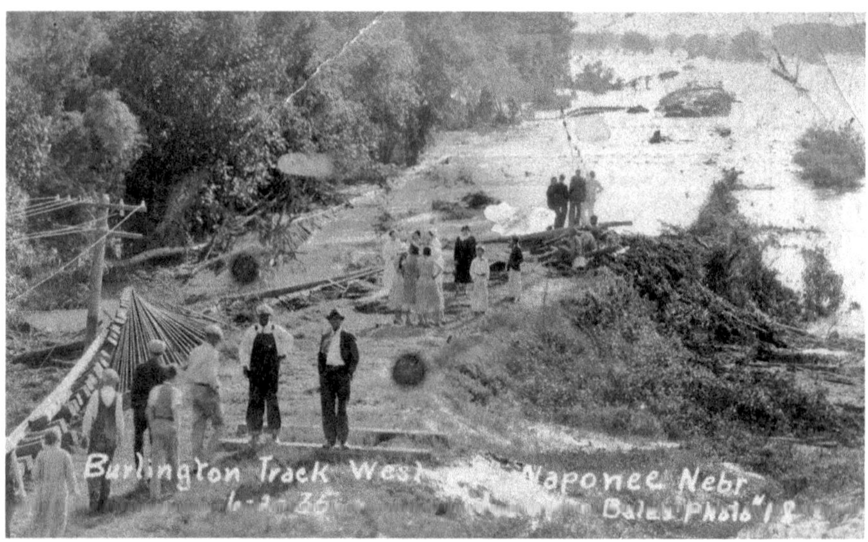

Burlington Track West, Naponee, Nebraska. *Joseph Torrey.*

him of the approaching flood. She asked him to send line rings to all of the people in his community. Clifford complied with the request and sent rings to everyone in the river bottom who had homes or property located there. The operator in Oxford called back with updates, which he relayed to local residents and to operators down the line every ten to twenty minutes. Those who answered found the stories hard to believe, especially lifetime residents of the area. Ever persistent, Clifford did not stop calling or sending men to check on families until he knew all had been moved to higher ground.

At 7:00 a.m., a replacement operator came to relieve Clifford. Clifford decided to see the flood for himself. He stood amazed outside the telephone office, watching as the immensity of the flood became a reality. Friends spotted him and hurried to tell him they had seen his brother trapped in a car overtaken by a wall of water and swept off the highway. Clifford ran up the highway searching for his brother. A neighbor stopped to give him a ride, and together they searched for Clifford's brother. To their immense relief, they soon found the boy, soaked to the skin and trembling, not too far up the road. Clifford's brother and his friends had abandoned the car and swam to the north and high ground. It would be two days before Clifford or his brother could get word to their parents to let them know they were both safe.

FRANKLIN

By the early hours of Saturday, June 1, 1935, urgent warnings were being dispatched to Franklin. Opal Miller Yelken was working at the Franklin Telephone Office that day. She took calls from telephone operators all along the Republican River that morning. However, calls from the west slowly ceased as telephone lines were destroyed by the flood. Opal made as many emergency line calls to everyone on shared telephone lines as she could. She warned everyone along the river of the coming danger, begging them to move to higher ground. She woke many families, persisting until lines went dead and Franklin was cut off from the rest of the world by the rising river. By noon, only the top of the arches could be seen on the new bridge, as the river had expanded to over two miles in width. Franklin lost Frank Greenleaf, Robert Miller and Will Watson.

RIVERTON

The skies cleared and the weather turned pleasant when the flood reached Riverton. Spectators lined both bluffs to watch the river roar past. Green fields were consumed by the torrential water, which swept by with houses, barns, fences, railroad tracks and trees caught in its embrace.

People on the banks were amazed by the awesome power of nature as they stood small and insignificant on the hills, watching as those still alive and trapped in the waters struggled to survive. Helplessness and despair soon replaced other emotions in the crowd as onlookers realized the malicious nature of the river. Bystanders were overcome with hopelessness as they watched the struggle for survival still going on in the lethal water.

RED CLOUD

Frank B. Achenial, secretary of the Nebraska Game and Parks Commission, was quoted in the June 2, 1935 *Denver Post* as saying:

> *Six weeks ago I stood on a hill here (in Red Cloud) in this fertile valley and watched a blinding dust storm sweep across it, tearing away its powdered soil. I am standing on the same hill today watching a wall of water sweep down, tearing everything in its path. I arrived at Red Cloud 4:00 p.m. The river was well within its banks. At 4:10 a dull roar could be heard, and ten minutes later a wall of water, four to 20 feet deep and two to three miles wide appeared. In 30 minutes fields, pastures, highways, the railroads—all was covered with black, surging, smelly water.*

On June 3, the local paper, the *Commercial Advertiser*, stated, "Practically the entire town was on hand to witness the arrival of the floodwaters, which carried along with it homes, barns, mammoth trees, livestock, and debris beyond description." Charles Stones recalled hearing a frightening roar and seeing buildings being pushed along by the floodwaters. They soon began to break up as they were pushed up against the trees, which also gave way to the force of the water.

GUIDE ROCK

Residents in Guide Rock flocked to the river to witness the spectacle. The roar of the waters could be heard for well over a mile before the river came into sight. Unfortunately, many people assembled on the bridge to watch the flood's approach. The *Guide Rock Signal* reported in its June 6, 1935 issue that a large group of people was waiting on the river bridge to watch for the expected flood. Realizing the danger, the sheriff forcibly removed the group, finally by gunpoint, to higher ground. Much grumbling and protesting was heard from those who felt they had been robbed of a perfect view of the flood. However, minutes later, the expected wall of water hit the bridge, sweeping it away. If not for the sheriff's action, the sightseers on the bridge would certainly have died.

Pawnee Lake, located two miles west of Guide Rock, vanished with the flood, consumed by the angry river. The river changed channels, creating the need for a new and larger bridge. One local man, Jim Jennings, stated that he lost everything but managed to find his appetite after two days' time.

SUPERIOR

The flood reached Superior, Nebraska, at 10:15 p.m. on Saturday, June 1. Due to both darkness and fog, the spectacle could not be seen—only heard, the rumble audible at 9:00 p.m. A reporter for the local paper, the *Superior Express*, stood with those who had come to witness the event. They waited at the cement plant and, with the aid of electric lights, watched the gauge on the trestle of the Burlington Railroad reveal the rising water. The gauge rose rapidly for forty-five minutes, but those watching did not realize the true height of the flood. The devious river cut out of its banks about a mile before it reached the plant, bypassing the trestle and eliminating about eight miles of the old riverbed. No west- or southbound trains or highway traffic entered the community for many days.

This did not stop the sightseers from coming to town. H.J. Nachtigall counted 160 cars in half an hour on the following Sunday afternoon. Residents estimated that fifteen thousand people came to town to see the flood. This provided local restaurant and gas station owners with their biggest day's business ever. One restaurant owner said he fed people constantly from lunch to dinner. This might have gone on longer, but an angry-looking cloud bank caused people to fear another storm, so they hurried home.

Chapter 10

BACK IN KANSAS

The Republican roared on, crossing the state line near Superior, Nebraska, and entering Kansas just after daylight. Perry Wilson, of Smith Center, heard about the flood and decided to travel east to see it for himself. He and Gus Beach stood on the riverbank as the flood roared by. The bank, undermined by the force of the waves, gave way, and the men were thrown into the river's angry clutches. A bystander pulled Beach from the water, but the river claimed Wilson as its own.

Rumors spread of a huge dam break somewhere in Colorado causing the flood. As the flood crests reached their communities, some heeded warnings, but many did not believe them. Kansans found it difficult to believe there could be much of a flood in the middle of such a severe drought. On June 3, the *Emporia Gazette* reported eleven people dead in Kansas. Where the Republican joined the Smoky Hill and Kaw Rivers at Junction City, the river ran at its all-time highest level.

Roads in Kansas closed due to mudslides, and floodwater left them piled high with debris. The city of Clyde became isolated from its neighboring communities. U.S. 81 north of Concordia washed away. Clay Center, Idana, Morganville and Clifton suffered extensive damage.

One of the final victims of the changeling Republican was Forrest Grooms of Clifton, Kansas. He planned to rescue others and lost his own life instead. He set out in a rowboat to assist in the rescue of nine Rock Island Railroad section men trapped by the rapidly rising water. Forrest's boat capsized. He clung to a telephone pole, awaiting rescue. Observers found his knife stuck in

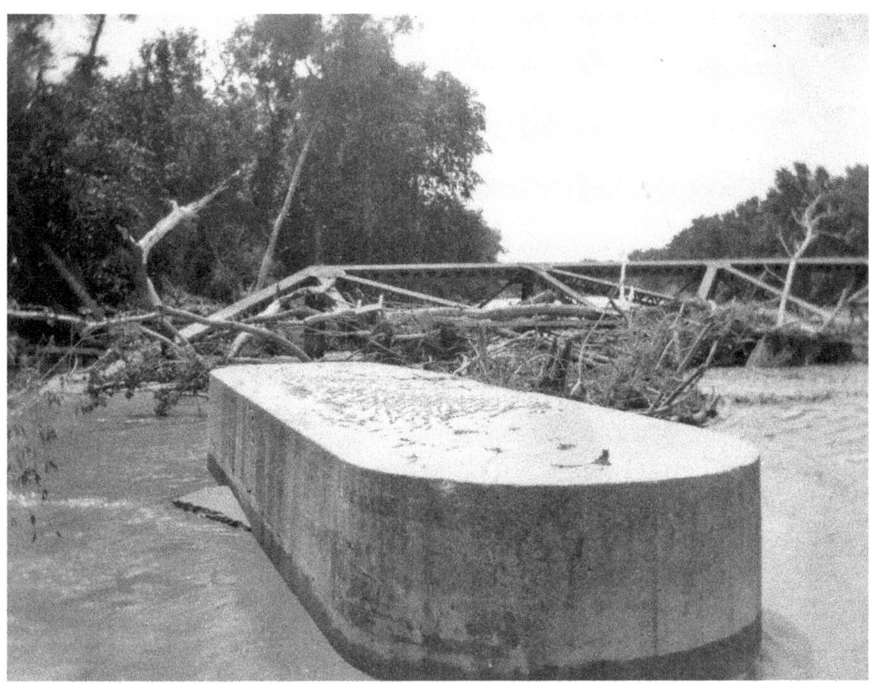

This bridge was snapped from its concrete base and tossed aside by raging water. *Joseph Torrey*.

the pole. They guessed he used it as a handle in order to hold on as the pole swayed in the surging water. Men in an approaching rescue boat heard him scream. Too late to help, their rescue turned into a recovery mission. The river finally gave up Forrest's body near Clay Center, over twenty miles away.

Soldiers from Fort Riley assisted local law enforcement and highway employees with keeping driftwood moving so that bridges would not be damaged by debris. The river at Milford rose eight feet in three hours to a stage five and a half feet over previously reported levels. The river swept away the town's Union Pacific station and eight boxcars located in a low-lying area.

Most of the Levi Carver family of rural Clyde, Kansas, located south and west of town on the Republican, were home when the floodwater reached their farm on June 2. Levi kept watch all night as the water began to rise. He left shortly after daylight to help another neighbor in town. When the first wave of high water hit the farm, his family jumped and ran for higher ground, with the angry floodwaters bearing down behind them.

A neighbor, Warren Payeur, who came to warn them of the wall of water making its way downriver, grabbed up the smaller children, Betty and

Maurice, as the high water approached the house. They rushed through a cornfield as the water lapped at their heels. He carried the children to a little rise, where they watched in horror as Eldon Carver ran through the cornfield carrying his mother, Ethel. The wall of water, a single cornrow behind the pair, seemed intent on swallowing them up as they rushed up the pasture hill.

They all made it to safety, and together they watched the river from their vantage point above their home. The river roared as though it was furious it had missed its intended victims. The family watched as the river swallowed their home and tossed it into a hole, dug by swirling tentacles of water. When they returned after the flood receded, they found their empty house in a thirty-foot-deep hole. The river had swept away the entire contents of the house. Kind neighbors provided the family with food and clothing until they could move to a new home on higher ground.

At the same time the Carvers were struggling to survive, several men were carried off the railroad tracks near Clyde. One, George LaBarge, struggled in the river for over fifteen miles before landing in a tree near Clifton. Many days passed before his family members knew if he had survived his struggle with the angry river.

CONCORDIA

In Concordia, the town newspaper stated in its weather column that Kansas was a state that had never had the right amount of water. In the summer of 1934, the Republican River bed lay completely dry. On June 1, 1935, the river stretched five miles wide and rose visibly throughout the morning. Farmers along the river bottom and in the north part of the city did not believe the flood could possibly be as bad as reported upstream, so many were taken by surprise when a three-foot wall of water came rushing through their property.

Earl Palmquist went along with Charles Campbell to help those trapped by the flood. They set out in a rowboat to help others but soon found that they were the ones in need of rescue. After spending a long night in a tree, they were brought out by motorboat.

The Harry Johnston family lived west of Concordia. Harry, his wife and two sons were in their family car when the flooding reached them about three miles from their home. The river overcame the car's engine, and the family abandoned it for higher ground nearby. They spent the night sitting under the insufficient shelter of some bushes, enduring hail and rain, before finally walking to a neighbor's farm for help.

Charles Blosser of Concordia spent hours in his plane warning the community and outlying farmsteads of the danger. He and his wife, Isabell, flew over the river to watch for the coming flood and were stunned to see the approaching wall of water between Guide Rock, Nebraska, and Norway, Kansas. From their vantage point in the air, they could see houses, barns, trees and cattle being forced along by the rampaging Republican.

Highway department employees, men from the sheriff's office and volunteers were trying to keep debris moving under the bridge north of Concordia. Charles and Isabell realized that the twenty or more men working the bridge would be in the direct path of the destruction. They flew back and warned them, but the men thought they would have time to complete clearing the debris before the high water reached their location. The Blossers watched helplessly as the river carried the bridge away, flinging the men into the water.

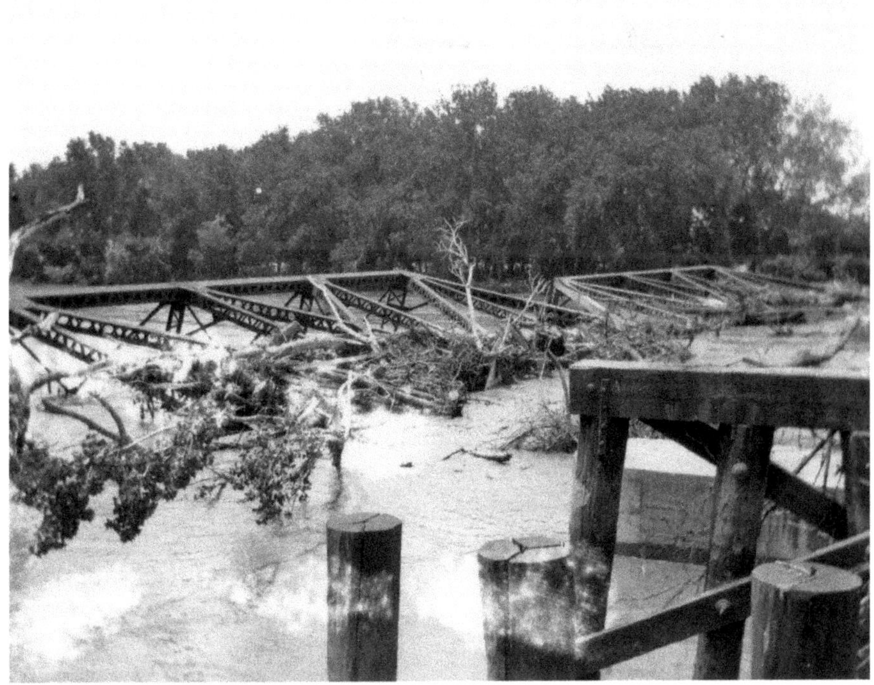

A bridge destroyed by the flood. *Joseph Torrey*.

Most of the men landed safely in a grove of catalpa trees, where they clung to the treetops. The Blossers contacted Martin Blosser, Charles's brother. Thanks to aerial observations and dedicated workers on the ground, Martin saved the stranded men with his large motorboat.

Over a period of four days, Charles used a hand-cranked siren to sound the alarm. When he spotted a group of people, he would cut his engine and fly low enough to shout instructions to aid in their rescue. As the waters receded, he helped in the rescue efforts, spotting survivors and dropping food and other packages to those cut off from their neighbors by the floodwaters. For one group, he dropped a rock with a note, asking them to stand apart so he could count how many people were stranded at that location. Later, he returned with a relief package, enough sandwiches for the entire group.

With no other transportation available, he shuttled people back and forth by air across the still-angry river. Blosser saved over twenty-eight people from the furious river during its rampage. He carried over one thousand passengers, including a ten-day-old baby. He ensured boats made it to the right locations and brought encouragement to stranded survivors. Largely due to his family's efforts, only four people died during the river's rampage through Concordia.

The Republican changed its course as it churned through Concordia and Clyde, abandoning two state bridges. On Highway 81, one of the bridges was so new that it had not yet been opened to traffic. Workers later spent weeks rerouting the Republican to again make use of both bridges.

CLAY CENTER

In 1934, less than a year before the flood, a photo of J.H. Kerby shows him standing in the Republican, a meager flow only ankle deep and less than seven feet wide. During the peak of the flood, the water rose more than twenty feet above flood stage at a depth of thirty to thirty-five feet.

According to an article in the *Clay County Times* on July 18, 1935, the river took the lives of three people, damaged three hundred buildings and homes and 15,000 acres of farmland and ruined 21,637 acres of growing crops. The ravenous river chewed out a new channel, drawing closer to the city than ever before.

During the flood, the local sheriff drove over 350 miles throughout the county, warning people of the impending disaster. He listened as residents repeatedly told him that the river had never reached their homes before. They told him they preferred to remain with their homes and property. This proved to be a disastrous decision for many in the valley.

Mail delivery proved to be especially difficult in the flooded community, as mailboxes were gone. In some locations, not only were the mailboxes missing, but so, too, were the homes and the highways leading to them. Mail carriers struggled for months to find people displaced by the flood.

Utility Park, one of the most picturesque spots in the city, suffered complete destruction. However, the fickle river left the ducks inhabiting the park untouched. They were in "duck heaven" with all the water in which they could swim.

The city water and light plant flooded to a depth of five feet, leaving the city without water and electricity for over twenty-four hours. A break in natural gas pipes also caused problems. Fuel had to be rerouted until the break could be repaired once the water returned to normal levels.

One local farmer, Ned Engler, reported that 160 acres of his river bottomland lay beneath a blanket of sand one to four feet deep. Like many farmers, Ned persisted. As an optimist, he always hoped for better luck next year. His personal tragedy was part of a news story in the *Clay Center Dispatch* on June 8, 1935. The paper noted that his farm had suffered "as much or more than anyone." The paper also reported that Ned planned to haul in some good black dirt and plant sweet clover to restore the soil. He believed his famous Engler watermelons would take root in the restored fields and thrive again.

WAKEFIELD

In Wakefield on the afternoon of June 3, three men were watching the flood from the river bridge. At about 5:00 p.m., the bridge began to sway. They heard the bridge begin to break up and rushed to the north side of the bridge. They were safe, but they watched as two spans toppled into the water, leaving them trapped until help arrived from Clay Center.

At Milford, Kansas, eight boxcars turned over, and the Union Pacific Depot washed off its site. Unlike its flooded neighbors, Milford stood high and dry, but it was completely cut off from surrounding communities. This left citizens without telephones or electricity, and they had a dwindling supply of meat and groceries. News from the community became limited to what a naval reserve officer relayed using a battery-operated shortwave radio.

Alida

Near Alida, the Republican cut an entirely new channel north of town. The water continued to rush on with the highest combined flow ever recorded for the Republican and Smoky Hill Rivers. The Republican joined the Kansas River at Junction City.

Junction City

The water rolled into Junction City at about 10:30 p.m. on June 3. The river spread to a width of three miles, stranding many in their farm homes. Warnings went out well in advance, and most fled to higher ground. Still, a few residents either refused to leave their homes or tried to cross the river too late. In the low-lying areas of the community, water rose to the tops of the first-floor windows and closed Highways 40 and 77, with levels over five feet deep on Highway 77. Highway 57 remained open, but the water came within a foot of the pavement. By 1:30 p.m., the flood had reached its peak. Later, a rise in the Smoky River caused renewed problems for the community.

Most people heard warnings about the flood, but some still refused to believe it could be as bad as reported. Thousands flocked to the riverbanks to see the floodwaters pass. One man, Corporal William Aleshire, walked out to meet his brother-in-law on Engineer's Bridge. When floodwaters overtook him, he spent over eight hours in a tree a half mile from dry land.

Manhattan

At Manhattan, downstream from Junction City, the Blue River, flowing in to the Kansas (or Kaw) River, rose slowly. A 4-H club in town watched the water flowing under and around the bridge over the Kaw. This river carried much of the debris from the Republican Valley, as well as most of the topsoil.

The *Colby Free Press* reported on June 12, 1935, that the 4-H leader put the group to work figuring out how much topsoil flowed along with the water going under the bridge. Using a bucket suspended on a rope, they dipped it into the water flowing under the bridge. After carefully weighing the bucket and evaporating the water inside, they calculated the width and depth of the water flowing under the bridge. They determined that a soil content of 699.3 acres per hour passed by their location. Almost 700 acres of topsoil, to a depth of one foot, swept from Kansas, Colorado and Nebraska fields by the crazed Republican moved swiftly east under the bridge.

The Rock Island Railroad lost its bridge and two miles of track near Manhattan. The highway known as the Midland Trail to Topeka washed out. Reports came in that one-third of the homes in Manhattan were surrounded by water. A report from Topeka on the same date listed all Kansas highways from Blue Rapids in the north, St. Francis in the far west and Medicine Lodge in south-central Kansas as closed because of high water. Many communities in between were isolated from their neighbors due to submerged or damaged bridges. Governor Alf Landon called a special meeting to determine what could be done to repair the damages that were crippling the state's transportation.

Heavy rain continued to fall across much of Nebraska and Kansas, causing flooding along the Solomon and Blue River Basins. Combined with floodwaters from the Republican and Kansas (Kaw) Rivers, all flowed swiftly into the Missouri River. By June 5, thousands were fleeing the lowlands along the Kansas and Missouri Rivers. Levees were strengthened to prevent overflow into the industrial districts of Kansas City. On June 7, reports of the passing of high water came in from Kansas City.

Here, the river seemed to tire, and the water no longer reached the crests it had attained upstream. A prison farm near Jefferson City, Missouri, was caught in the rising water and the inmates forced to evacuate; 1 convict drowned as the other 139 moved through the floodwaters to high ground. Standing Rock, east of Columbia, Missouri, on the Katy Trail, still bears the mark of the high water of 1935. The rampage of the Republican River begun so far away in Colorado had finally ended. After sweeping over seven hundred miles through four states, it resumed its placid ways, once again a silent river meandering through the plains.

Chapter 11

Aftermath

Flying low like a hawk the aircraft sailed across scenes of utter devastation that no pen could describe nor cameras do justice to. Farms were swept clean of topsoil, replaced by sand covered in slime. Railroad tracks were twisted and thrown off their beds. Houses were completely destroyed or remained tilting and turned on their foundations. In an area two hundred miles in length and from one to three miles wide, dead horses, cattle, and hogs lay rotting in the sun. And on the horizon dust clouds gathered, signs of another dust storm sweeping down from the west." This was the account printed by the *McCook Daily Gazette* on June 3, 1935, the reporter's reaction following a plane trip over the devastation.

During the days when the flood scoured the land, beautiful expanses of meadowland became a barren desert, a land of sand. Every breeze shifted the sand around the sodden piles of debris. The overwhelming smell of rotting flesh from the dead sickened rescuers and cleanup crews. It would be winter before the smell froze away.

Workers began to tally the dead and homeless. Very few survivors had anything with which to start again. Many had been warned, but few listened; as a result, they lost all personal property. In spite of this, the valley people determined to begin again—men and women worked as they had never worked before. As Joe Fleming wrote in his memoirs, "Much work needed to be done and all of it needed to be done first." The land needed to be cleared, crops needed to be replanted, homes needed to be cleaned out or

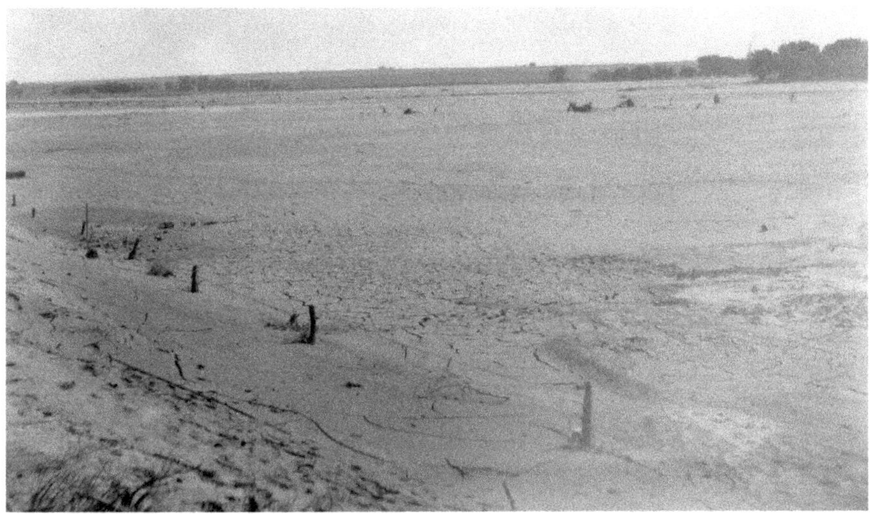

Mud-covered fields after the flood. *Joseph Torrey.*

rebuilt, livestock needed to be recovered and highways and bridges needed to be rebuilt.

In the weeks after the flood, Lloyd Harvey of McCook drove all over the area, delivering freight in his truck. He heard many tales of the harrowing ordeals people had gone through. One family told of water coming up so fast it rushed in the house as they dashed up the stairs to the second floor. The water followed them, reaching the second story before they did. Some people had to break out the windows of their single-story homes to escape when the water rushed in and trapped them with water almost as high as the ceiling. Others told of the long hours they spent in trees, some stranded for as much as seventy-two hours awaiting rescue.

All along the river, cooking pans, quilts and clothing were found as high as twenty-five feet above the ground in the surviving trees. Workers discovered a live hog twenty feet above the ground downriver from its farm home. The flood also deposited hundreds of snakes buried in the sand. When residents returned to their homes, they found snakes coming out of the kitchen cabinets.

Despite warnings from local law enforcement, looters often took anything useable found along the riverbanks or stuck in treetops. Some, pretending to help, loaded the belongings they helped recover into their own cars and drove away, never to be seen again.

At first, very little news of the tragedy made its way to the outside world. People struggled to help their nearest neighbors. Lloyd went as far west as

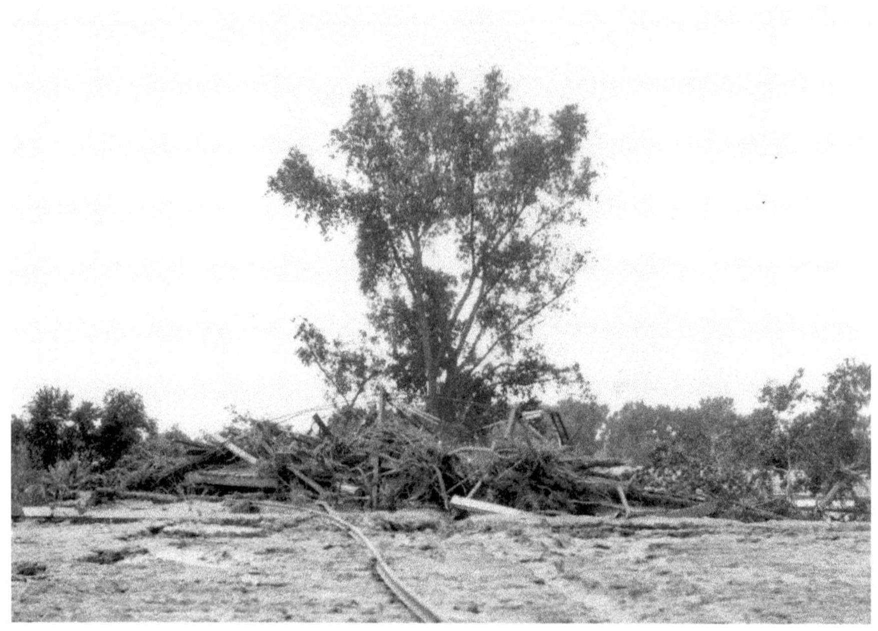

Debris piled around a bridge near Orleans, Nebraska. *Joseph Torrey*.

Colorado; as far south as Oberlin and St. Francis, Kansas; and as far east as Oxford, Nebraska. All of the roads along his route had suffered heavy damage, and detours were necessary for many months. Treeless riverbanks were stripped of all vegetation, and only white sand remained. The valley turned into a veritable desert, complete with sandstorms. Never had he seen the valley look so hopeless.

The search for those lost in the flood began immediately. Airplanes flew over the area, attempting to spot stranded residents. After a time, no more survivors could be found, and the grim task of identifying bodies began. Funeral homes were lined with the coffins of those who had perished. In some places, entire families simply disappeared, sucked under the crush of sand and debris.

Hampered by the remaining floodwater, some people were unable to get to town for over six weeks. Dangers lurked in the areas where bodies were found, as rattlesnakes had collected by the thousands, taking refuge in the bluffs among the uprooted trees. Some people became ill with food poisoning after eating from contaminated stored food. Georgia Hellner remembered her mother saying that her dreams of a comfortable income, a modern home and college for her children were halted by

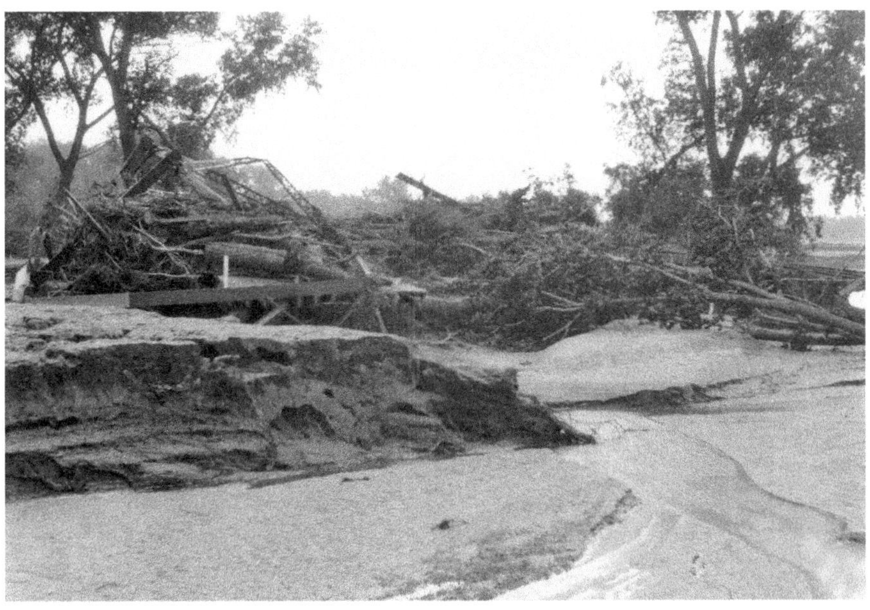

Mud and debris piled high made cleanup difficult. *Joseph Torrey*.

the Depression, blown away by the dirt storms and finally washed away completely by the deluge on the Republican.

Ralph Best remembered that while his family was working in the fields, someone drove into their yard and took their new harnesses out of the barn. The thieves left evidence that they did not use the harnesses for their intended purpose. Instead, they cut them up to wrap around their car tires so they could drive back out of the muddy farmyard. After that terrible experience, Ralph's father hired a guard to keep watch on their home whenever they were away.

Estimates of over five thousand sightseers looking over the ruins of the flood were reported in a single day in Cambridge. Milo Whiteman said he counted eighty-seven people walking through his house on the south side of Cambridge within five minutes. People longed to help, to find missing family, to do something for someone—anyone. Unfortunately, there were few swept into the flood who could be saved, and little could be done except to help as residents began to rebuild.

The now-placid river returned to its new channels and cross channels. Farm families often found their most productive fields at the bottom of the new riverbed. Some discovered that the river had left their farms sliced apart, with the farmhouse on one side of the river and the outbuildings and

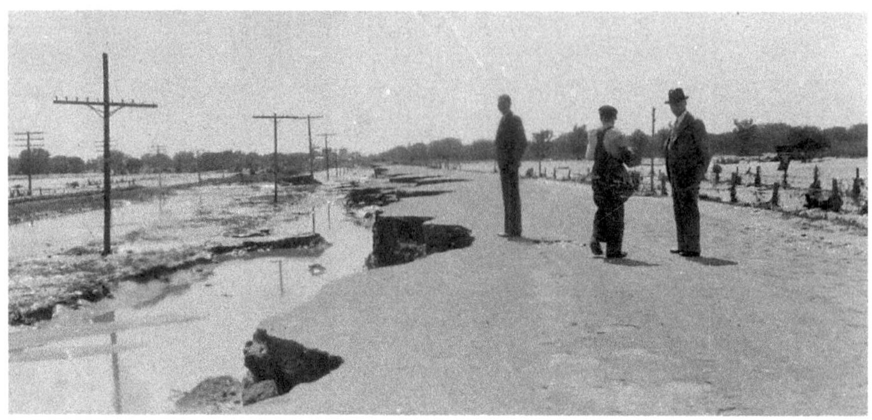

An inspection of the damaged highways following the flood. *Cambridge Museum.*

corrals on the other. Andy Gibson in Trenton discovered his farm on an island in the middle of an entirely new channel, a less than ideal location.

Quicksand, a danger at every turn, remained a problem the entire summer. A layer of slime deposited on everything the water touched fouled the air with its stench. One woman living near Max, Nebraska, went out after the flood to see what she could find to salvage. She saw a shoe sticking up in the mud, gave it a tug and found a leg attached. She discovered later that the leg belonged to Ora David. One of the river's victims, his body had traveled over three and a half miles from his last known location. The river had covered his body with sand and slime and placed him right next to the house in the unlucky woman's vegetable garden.

Archie Burke tried to assist in the cleanup. He hoped to find the body of his daughter, Lois. The crews used pitchforks to clear the piles of debris because so many snakes hid within their depths. Burke could not bring himself to use his pitchfork. He cringed every time he put the fork into a pile of debris for fear of striking his little girl's body. Moved by his loss and grief, community leaders assigned him to different work. Days would turn into weeks as the hunt continued for the missing.

Haunted by the screams of those trapped during the deluge, Dot Blincow Manley, of Edison, Nebraska, like so many others in the area, could never bring herself to live close to the river again. The memories of the terrible stench and the nightmares about the men she saw perish would drive her permanently to higher ground.

Officials called on the military to establish an air base for flood recovery operations in North Platte, Nebraska. North Platte also became the center of operations for the Federal Emergency Relief Administration (FERA) and the Red Cross as area leaders scrambled to bring food, clothing and household goods to affected families.

Work began immediately to reestablish communications. At first, the local phone companies were swamped with calls. A new problem arose as people found working telephones and made calls to let relatives know they were still alive. Lines became so busy that operators instructed customers to limit their long-distance calls to three minutes per person each evening. Hundreds toiled to restore highways and railroads. Jobs were created as residents found work helping to restore the infrastructure of their communities.

Materials and men were trucked in to start repair work on the railroad and telephone lines. In a 1985 interview, W.H. Mengel recalled working on the highway surveys after the flood: "A day or two after the Republican River Valley flood, I was told to stop the job I was on near David City and go to the McCook Division and start some surveys to relocate Highway 6 because of the flood damage. My first assignment was at Cambridge. I also had to go up and down the river and get an inventory of the damage to the bridges over the Republican." Adding to the difficulty of this task were the dust storms that continued to sweep in from the west.

Camps appeared everywhere as spring turned to summer. These camps were located near communities where the men were working. Most had a camp superintendent and a timekeeper. Men and boys lived in tents, with their meals served in their new tent cities. The *McCook Tribune* reported that one thousand Civilian Conservation Corps (CCC) men were allocated to McCook to help with the cleanup. "Many a boy has tossed away his breakfast on the sandbar and gone right back to the job," said William T. Dunn, superintendent of the CCC camp, who was leading the campaign to get rotten carcasses of drowned animals buried as quickly as possible. Trucks also brought in his men to hunt for human bodies and perform other emergency sanitation work.

These large forces of men traveled up and down the riverbanks spreading quick lime, hurrying to bury the dead to prevent the spread of disease. The odor of the rotting flesh and the swarming of flies made the gruesome job even more unpleasant. The CCC and FERA brought an additional 1,600 men to the area, some of whom stayed to make their homes in the places they worked.

Farmers applied to their local county extension agents for assistance from the CCC. Upon approval from a board consisting of the county agent, a Red Cross representative and the rehabilitation supervisor for CCC and FERA,

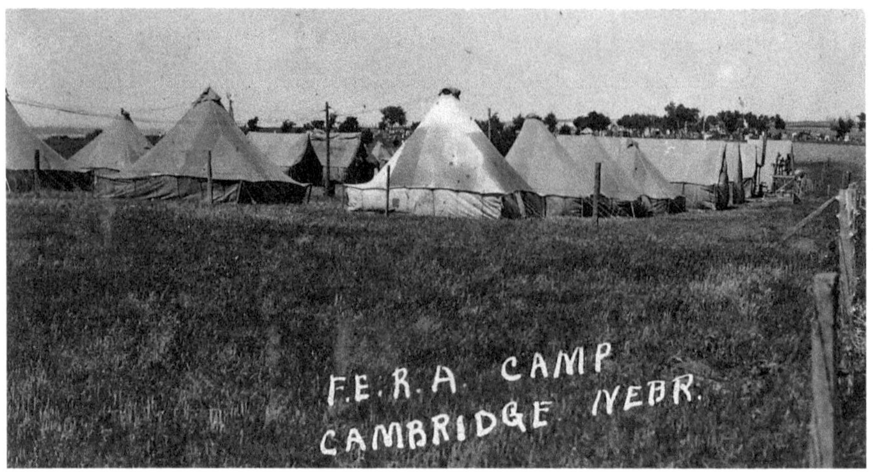

The FERA camp near Cambridge. *Cambridge Museum.*

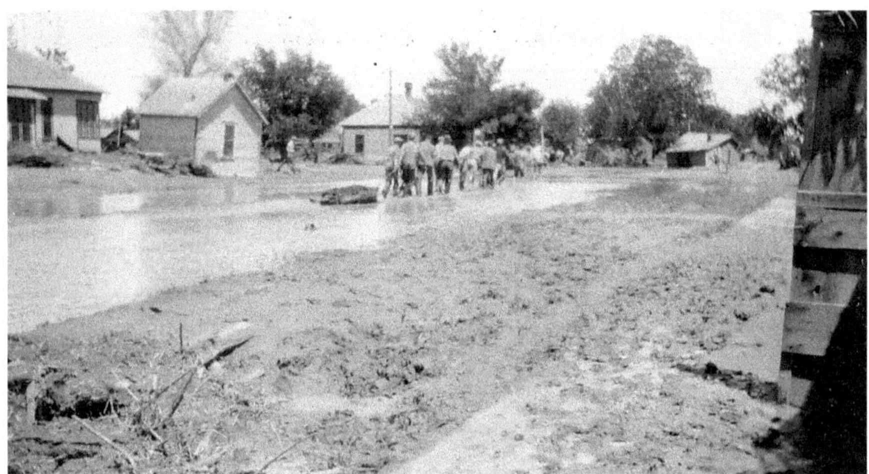

CCC boys aid in cleanup efforts by removing a dead animal. *Cambridge Museum.*

the men and boys would go to work restoring the farmer's land to pre-flood conditions. Jo Krug Mann remembered that her sister complained that she didn't do her share of the cleanup at their home when the CCC came to help them after the flood. Irene pointed out that because many of the young men were only fifteen or sixteen years old, Jo spent more time watching them than she did doing her share of the cleaning.

At the end of the relief activity, the Red Cross reported that its costs totaled over $167,000. Half of this money came from its treasury and the other half from local donations. The organization was assisted by the CCC, the army and military medical officers. Also assisting were Boy Scouts who acted as messengers and guides.

The Red Cross set up lost-and-found centers and typhoid inoculation centers. These centers were vital to prevent diseases that could flourish in the unsanitary conditions prevalent in the area due to the hundreds of dead livestock and other dead animals trapped in the debris. This significant danger lessened as quick action kept the population safe. Orders to boil all water went out across the area and were not lifted until the water could be confirmed safe for drinking and bathing. Reports of smallpox came in from Benkelman, and a call went out for a vaccine. Those suffering from the disease—nine in all—were isolated from the general population, and a possible epidemic was averted.

After the flood, local newspapers were filled with all kinds of advertisements and public announcements. One farmer filed a classified ad asking for help in locating seventeen heifers and thirteen calves lost west of McCook. Clark's Style Shoppe, at 217 Main, advertised "Flood Values" with silk dresses for $2.95. According to the *McCook Tribune*, gasoline was sold by permit only in McCook due to the limited supply.

Perhaps Eglantine Berger's letter to her husband, Stuart, best described Cambridge after the flood. In her letter, Eglantine stated:

> *Tonight we fed the refugees for the last time—81 of them. They are getting settled and can prepare the food, if the Red Cross furnishes it for them...They all seemed very grateful, and I'm sure they are—I know I'd appreciate any kindness under such circumstances, and perhaps I'll need it someday as much as these people do now. The first day was just terrible from start to finish—people came in looking like ghosts, people who couldn't eat, people who no longer owned a change of clothing; people bare footed and with tear-stained faces and voices that trembled when they asked for "just a cup of coffee, please." You dared not offer sympathy and comfort, for their hearts were full to bursting and they couldn't stand it. Many were wet to the armpits from the rescue...And worst of all were the ones who had people on the south side of river and got no word from them 'til Sunday...The National Red Cross worker came in Monday and these people will be helped by them; helped to get a new start perhaps and in time I think they will think of this terrible disaster with different feelings...It's worth your time to see this country now. The bottom land looks like a desert.*

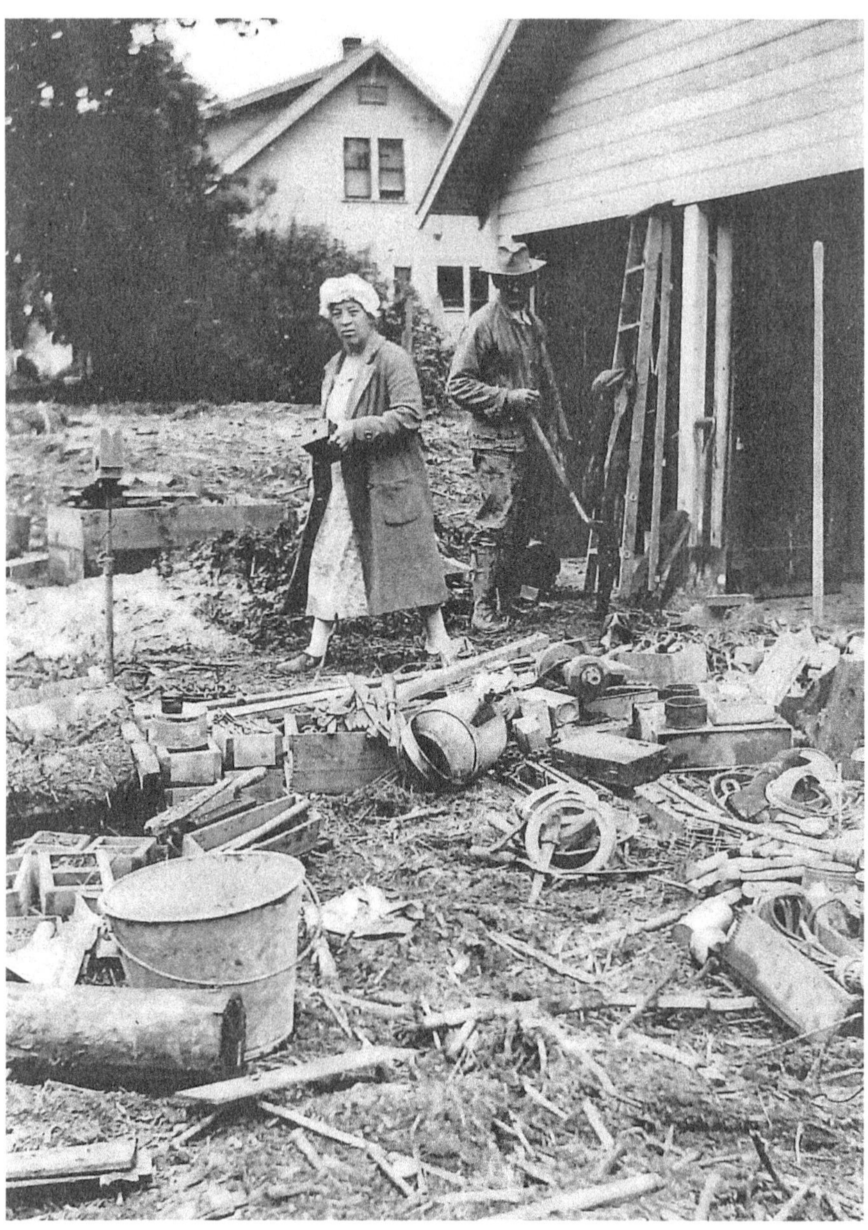

Cleanup after the flood was a dirty and dangerous business. *Cambridge Museum.*

Owners of flood-damaged property were faced with the monumental task of cleaning out several feet of mud and debris and then washing everything in their homes. Often, all their possessions—if they could even be found—would be hanging in treetops or buried in the mud. Families found every crevice in their homes filled with mud. One housewife found all her silverware scattered outside her house for hundreds of feet in every direction.

Home Building Savings & Loan of McCook prepared a statement about property values. A farm appraised at $1,500 before the flood sold shortly after the high water for $150. Another previously valued at $4,500 sold for just $25.

After three days, restoration of minimal electric power came to McCook when the generators were hooked up again in the open air on high ground. Thanks to the foresight of the workers at the McCook Power Plant, who had wrapped the three generators with burlap before the flood, they could be placed back into service quickly. Although the burlap hadn't kept the water out, it did keep out the mud. One motor quickly put into service generated enough power for city residents. However, local papers like the *Tribune* reminded residents to use all electrical devices sparingly until full service returned.

Engineers from as far away as Washington State helped get the plant in McCook back into service. They found the collapsed electric plant filled with mud, along with trees and carcasses of dead animals, which included a cow, a coyote and, according to one report, a small mountain lion. On June 22, 1935, they determined that the plant would be rebuilt on higher ground. The first engine for the new plant began operation within forty-seven days. This and the additional motors needed to power the community stood in the open air until the completion of the new plant in 1938.

Although McCook residents at first had to boil water, a chlorinator hooked up to the water system at a cost of $1,500 solved this problem, according to the *McCook Tribune*'s city council report. The chlorinators "will not prove harmful if used commercially but might hasten the action of home brew," explained a councilman.

Reinstallation of communication lines took weeks. Limited news came from radio reports and telegrams received by railroad depot agents. They passed along new information to local residents and newspapers. Rumors ran rampant until official communications could be restored. One rumor caused some families much worry. It was reported that the entire city of St. Francis lay covered in water. Relatives and friends were frantic with worry until actual reports of the conditions there came out of the Kansas valley.

Men previously unemployed found work with the railroads. Hundreds of miles of track, roadbeds and bridges needed to be rebuilt. Local papers

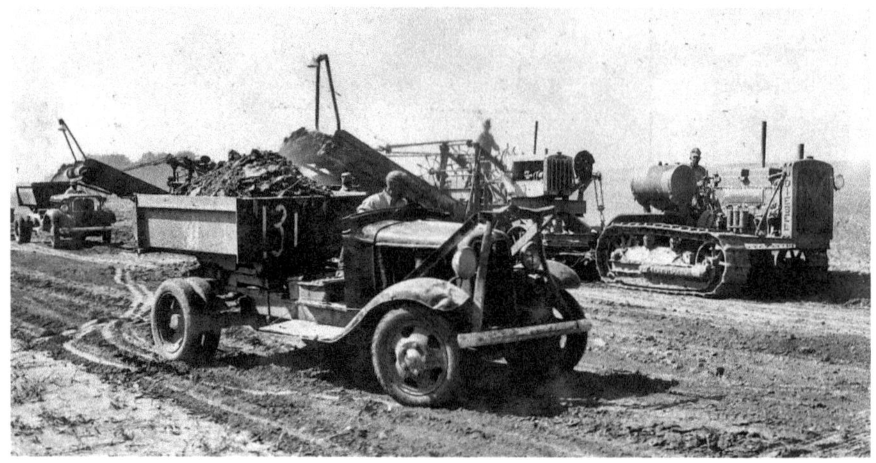

Construction to replace the damaged highways begins. *Cambridge Museum.*

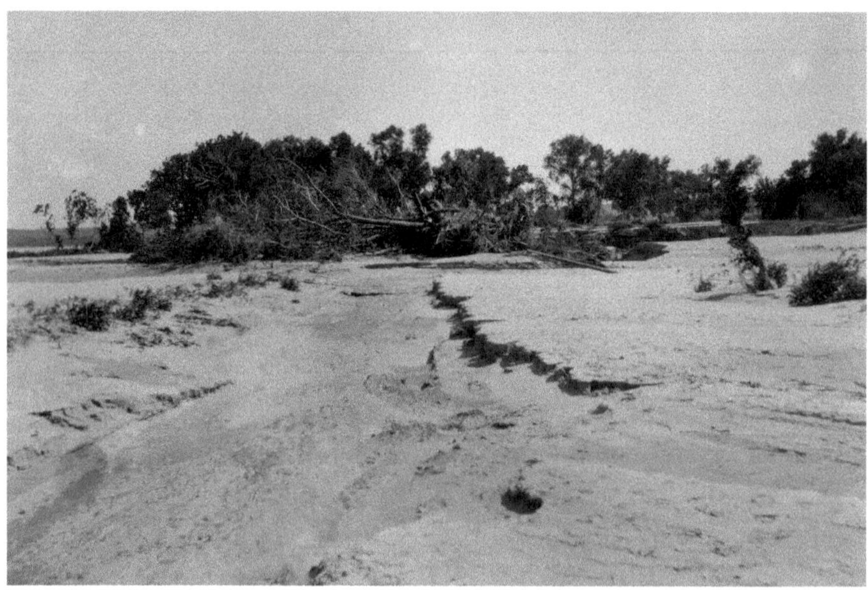

Drifts of sand covered farmers' fields after the flood. *Joseph Torrey.*

advised job seekers to check at the local train depot and at their city and county offices to obtain work.

Farmers went to their fields to begin cleanup. In Trenton, their property near the river lay beneath a coat of sand and mud up to two feet in depth. In other areas, the deep sand created a desert where rich meadows had once thrived.

It would be years before anything could be grown on these fields. Fleas and mosquitoes infested the area and made life miserable for both men and wildlife until the killing frost of fall. Housewives fought mud from the fields, dust from the sky and insects that swarmed into their homes and refused to leave.

The June 10, 1935 edition of the *Omaha World Herald* stated that the area around McCook was beginning to show signs of improvement from cleanup efforts. Near Cambridge, where damage had been much more extensive, the paper stated that residents were still in a state of shock, as the losses in life and property were almost overwhelming. Requests for relief were being processed by the governor's office. The Red Cross fed and clothed over one thousand people there. Still, many refused assistance, too proud to accept any kind of help.

Ernest Purvis, twelve years old at the time of the flood, lived with his family between Medicine Creek and the Republican. While he and his father went to watch the Republican flood on the south side of Cambridge, Medicine Creek flooded, moving their house from its foundation. In an interview in 2011, Ernest told his son Tom that the house and its foundation were not tied together by plumbing or electrical lines, as the family did not enjoy either of these luxuries. So when the water came, the house simply floated away.

The Purvis family, like most others in Cambridge, could not afford to move or to build again. Ernest's father thought of a creative solution to their problem. He attached leather straps to their home and, using mules, pulled the house back to its original location. The Purvises, like hundreds of

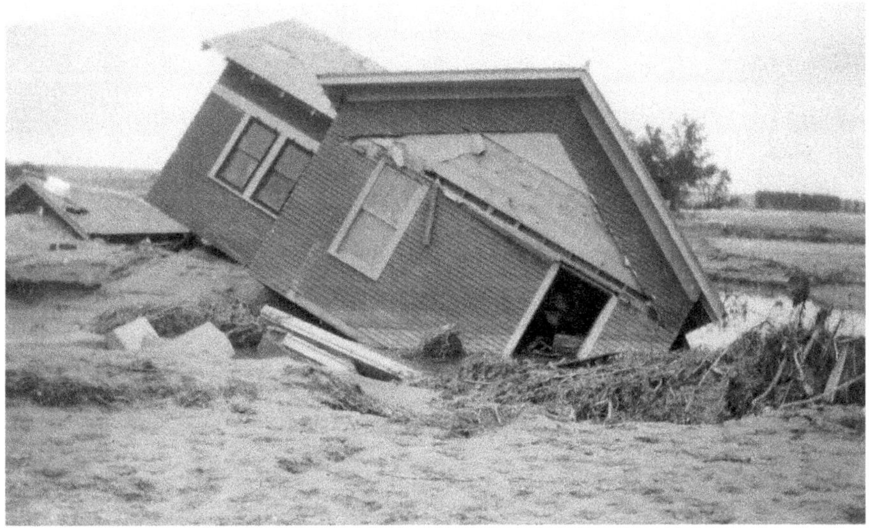

A destroyed home. *Nebraska Prairie Museum.*

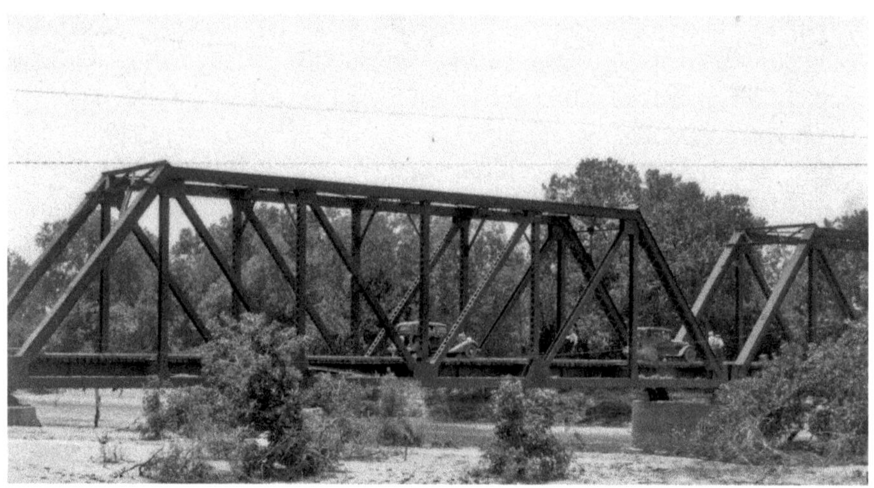

Cars using a railroad bridge to cross the river after the flood. *Joseph Torrey*.

others, began the massive work of cleaning out the mud and debris, washing everything from ceiling to floor and attempting to salvage anything not totally destroyed by the foul waters.

Bridges were among the first things that needed to be replaced so that highway and rail travel could be resumed. After the flood, no bridges spanned the river for hundreds of miles. Not long before the flood, a new bridge had been built on the river at Franklin, Nebraska. The construction included a detailed survey of the riverbed. A similar survey taken shortly after the flood revealed the entire riverbed scoured down to the shale. This was thirty feet below the original streambed. All clay soil in the river was replaced with sand and gravel. In addition, a one-hundred-foot span of the bridge lay buried beneath the gravel. A special pier had to be designed during the construction of the replacement bridge to avoid this large obstacle, making rebuilding a great challenge.

In Nebraska alone, forty-one road and bridge projects were needed to replace state and federal bridges in the flood zone. County bridges became the responsibility of the local governments. An article in one local paper stated that any able-bodied man could find work, as so many were hiring men to repair the damages throughout the valley.

R.S. Otis stated on May 31, 1935, "We were dried out last year. This year blown out, drowned out, burned up, and we are still here able to kick. And we have a kick a coming. Great praise is due the brave people who lost their all. They smile and go on living, but we know their hearts are sad."

FLOOD DATA FOR COLORADO AND NEBRASKA

Table adapted from data recorded in
High Water Mark *by Raymond Borchers*

Location	Depth in Feet	Width in Feet	Width in Miles	Casualties
North Fork	3.5	2,640	0.5	
Arikaree	11.2	1,214.4	0.23	5
Haigler	13	1,425.6	0.27	
Parks	17	2,481.6	0.47	1
South Fork	14	3,062.4	0.58	
Benkelman	19	5,438.4	1.03	22
Max	13.8	5,808		
Stratton	14	4,963.2	0.94	3
Trenton	16	5,544	1.05	9
Culbertson	12	7,920	1.5	
Republican W of McCook	14	8,500.8	1.61	10
Republican E of McCook	29	1,161.6	2.2	
Red Willow	23.9	1,636.8	0.31	
Indianola	22	5,702.4	1.08	
Bartley	17	7,075.2	1.34	
Medicine	18.6	1,003.2	0.19	
Cambridge	20	8,976	1.7	3
Edison	21	7,972.8	1.51	6
Oxford	18	8,712	1.65	17
Orleans			1.65	16
Alma	25	7,339.2	1.39	1
Bloomington	20.4	6,072	1.15	
Franklin	20	6,072	1.15	3
Riverton	25	6,652.8	1.26	
Red Cloud	24	6,336	1.2	
Guide Rock	24	7,128	1.35	
Superior	14	8,553.6	1.62	

*Casualties listed above differ from other accounts due to a lack of information available at the time of Borchers's research.

Chapter 12

NEVER AGAIN!

It seemed as if all eyes turned to the Republican Valley following the flood. Almost every major newspaper in the United States ran a story about the flood rampaging in the heartland during the Dust Bowl. People began to ask the questions that would change the heartland and the Republican River Valley. What can we do about the dust storms and erosion? What can we do to tame the rivers and stop the terrible spring floods? What can we do to improve the infrastructure of our communities? How can we bring communications and electricity to the farm families of our country?

Citizens of the area worked tirelessly to rebuild their communities. Reflecting the courage and self-reliance of their pioneer parents, men and women in the region banded together to rebuild. Sweeping change would soon follow.

Some believe the flood acted as the hinge on the door opening into the future. On one side of the door, the old ways of the nineteenth century clung to the area. The flood swept all of that away, leaving the door open to change. Waiting on the other side were more modern transportation and communication methods and mechanized farming practices. The countryside, and the lives of those who inhabited the country, would never be the same.

Governor R.L. Cochran of Nebraska conferred with President Franklin Roosevelt and reached an agreement to provide relief for stricken families. Immediate assistance became available to provide basic livestock to farm families, seed for forage crops and assistance to rebuild their homes.

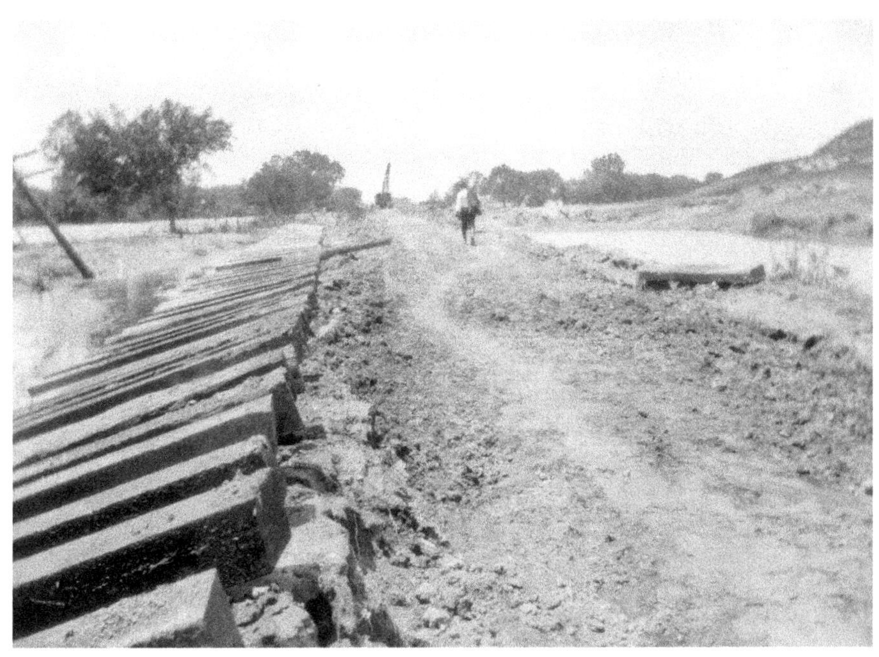

An unidentified man going to work repairing the railroad in Nebraska. *Joseph Torrey*.

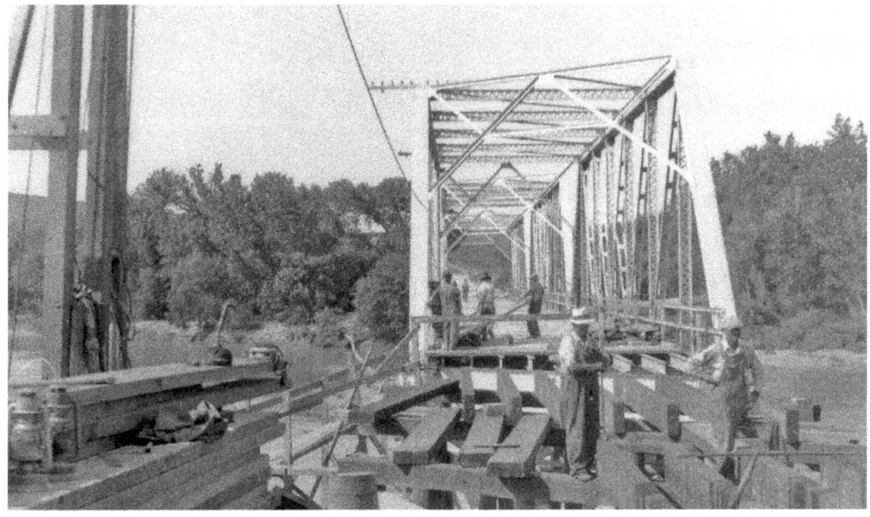

Building a new bridge. *Joseph Torrey*.

Governor Alf Landon of Kansas pinpointed the areas of drought and flood within his state and begged for water and soil conservation measures throughout the state.

Requests for cash assistance were met by federal, state and private donations. A total of $710,800 was needed to repair roads in Furnas, Hayes, Frontier, Red Willow and Hitchcock Counties in Nebraska. Each highway river bridge cost approximately $70,000 and each small stream bridge about $25,000 to repair. In the McCook, Nebraska area alone, the American Red Cross received requests from 1,202 valley families for assistance after the flood. Later reports indicated that of the 1,202 families requesting help, 790 reestablished themselves and continued to live and work in the valley. A sketch in area papers showed the kind of homes provided for those who had lost everything in the flood. The floor plan of these modest frame houses included one bedroom, a kitchen and a living room.

Harry Strunk, owner of the *McCook Daily Gazette*, vowed that his community would never again suffer the loss of life and property that he had witnessed on May 31, 1935. He worked tirelessly to make this change a reality. As president of the Republican Valley Conservation Association, he promoted his campaign for flood control. He spoke with thousands of area residents and spent countless hours visiting with officials ranging from local county clerks all the way to White House personnel and the president of the United States. With the motto "Service is the rent we pay for the space we occupy in this world," he saw positive change come to the area in his lifetime.

Senator George Norris of Nebraska flew immediately to the scene of the disaster. Horrified by what he saw, he determined that Nebraska did not need public assistance; it needed public works. His plan included rebuilding the area and protecting it from future catastrophes. He also championed the rural electrification program, which would bring sweeping change to local farms.

Some called attention to the area in other ways. A cottonwood tree near the highway crossing in Benkelman, Nebraska, had been turned upside down in the floodwaters. Its branches had become firmly planted in the sand, with its roots spread out twelve feet above. People stopped to have their pictures taken with the oddity. Robert Ripley, of Ripley's Believe It or Not fame, found the picture intriguing and ran it in his column, which appeared in many major newspapers. Millions saw the photo and learned what had happened in Nebraska following the flood.

Another person who took it upon himself to call attention to the flood was D.F. Neiswanger. Neiswanger worked as a stonecutter in Cambridge and, as a hobby, erected monuments marking the location of historically

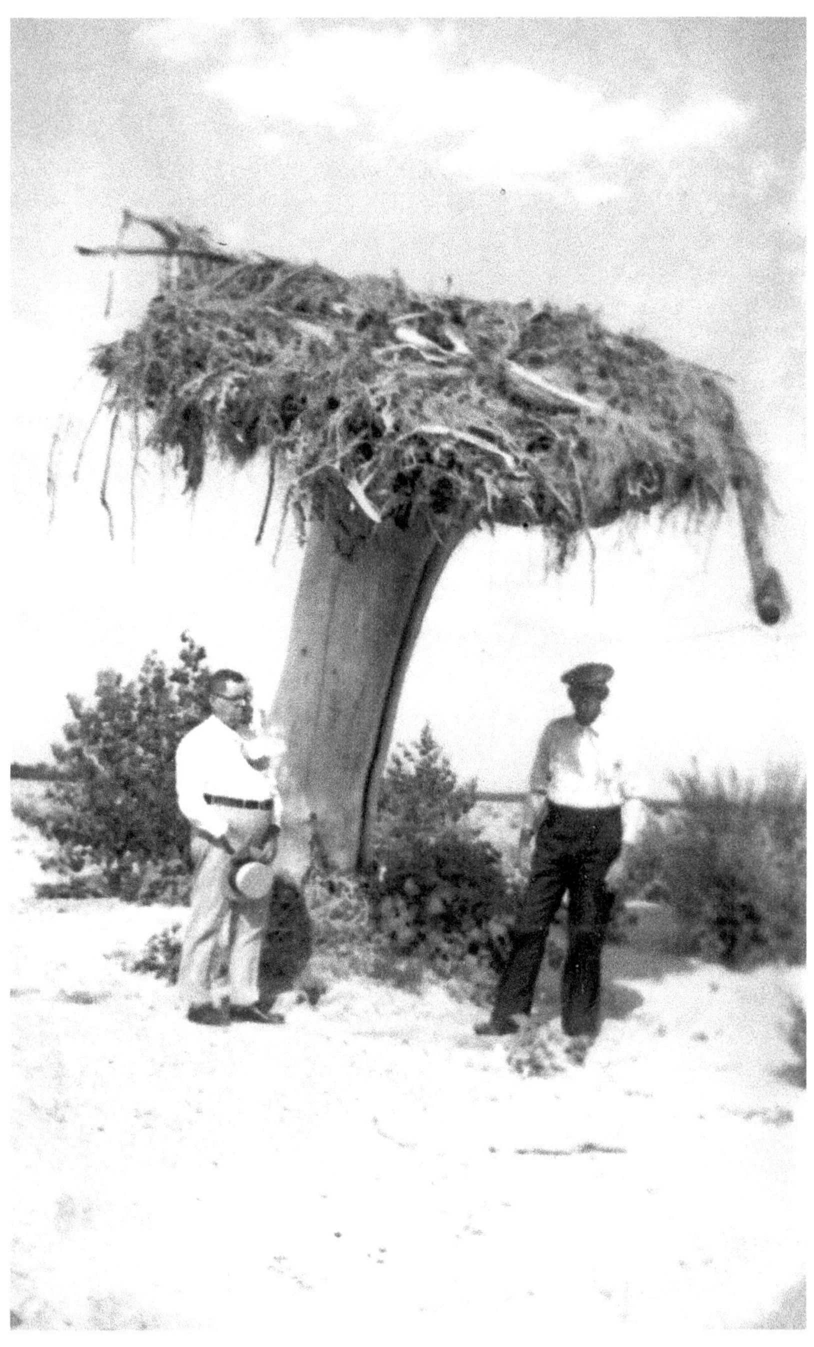

An upside-down cottonwood tree in Benkelman, Nebraska. *Lucille Edwards.*

significant events in his area. Neiswanger, also a student of human nature, realized that people would soon forget the flood or would argue about the location of the high-water marks in their communities. In the *Cambridge Clarion* on January 23, 1936, Neiswanger was quoted as saying that in future years, "people would probably guess, wonder and argue as to the highest point the water reached." To prevent this from happening, he placed eight markers documenting the flood in 1936. As of this writing, seven remain as a testament to the foresight of this local historian.

Additionally, landowners, businessmen and local government officials began demanding assistance from the federal government. The Departments of Agriculture, Interior and War responded, conducting surveys in the area. Charles Blosser of Concordia worked with the Bureau of Reclamation and Senator Frank Carlson of Kansas in bringing flood control to Kansas. Intensive investigations initiated in 1939 and continued during the succeeding years provided the foundation for a plan for controlling floods and storing water for irrigation. This plan, published as Senate Document 191, included the overall development of the Missouri River Basin.

The Bureau of Reclamation began work in the area in 1939. Its initial investigations were completed and reported on in March 1940. Army engineers gave orders to begin a survey along the Nebraska portion of the river to determine the feasibility of a reservoir system. Colorado, Kansas and Nebraska entered into an agreement with the federal government in 1943 to divide the water equitably.

The public's demand for flood control during Senator Norris's time in Congress led to his one considerable success, the Flood Control Act of 1944, more commonly known as the Pick-Sloan Act. This act brought public works to his home state of Nebraska and authorized a series of dams to be built along the Republican and its tributaries. With the construction of the dams came opportunities for irrigation, recreation, wildlife conservation and reduction of pollution in small streams. On April 8, 1946, the Frenchman-Cambridge Irrigation District formed, and on November 1, 1946, the first contract was awarded for the construction of Enders Dam.

Construction of the division started on March 1, 1947. The Cambridge and Medicine Creek Dams were completed in 1949, the Enders Dam in 1951, the Trenton Dam in 1953, the Bartley Diversion Dam in 1954, the Culbertson Diversion Dam in 1959 and the Red Willow Dam in 1962. The Cambridge and Bartley Canals were completed in 1954, the Driftwood Canal in 1959, the Red Willow Canal in 1964, the Culbertson Canal Enlargement in 1961 and the Culbertson Extension Canal in 1961.

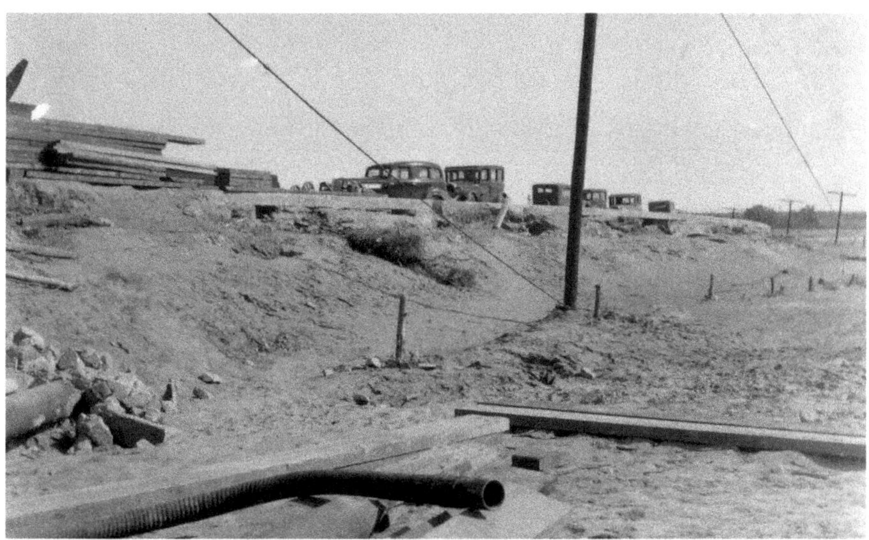

Rebuilding the highway. *Joseph Torrey*.

There have been several other dams constructed in the Republican Basin, most in response to the 1935 flood. As part of the Missouri River Basin flood control and land reclamation project, the other dams include the Harlan County Dam (1948) near Alma, Nebraska, and the Milford Dam (1965) near Junction City, Kansas. Republican tributaries that erected flood control structures included Bonny Dam (1951) near Burlington, Colorado; Enders (1951) and Medicine Creek (Harry Strunk Lake, 1949) in Nebraska; and Lovewell (1957) near Mankato, Kansas.

According to the history of the Bostwick Division, "On March 19, 1941, representatives of Colorado, Nebraska, and Kansas agreed upon and signed a Republican River compact hailed as the first step toward a peaceful settlement of long drawn out and expensive water controversies between the three states. The compact had the effect of fixing limits to which any of the three states could go in depleting the water supply of the Republican River basin. Its objective was to permit development to go forward in the three states within the limit of the allocated water supplies without danger of future litigation." The water of the Republican seemed equally divided among the states, ensuring equal water rights for all.

A serious flood in June 1947 reinvigorated the push to control the Republican. Fueled by postwar optimism and an increased demand for irrigation, construction of dams and reservoirs along the Republican began

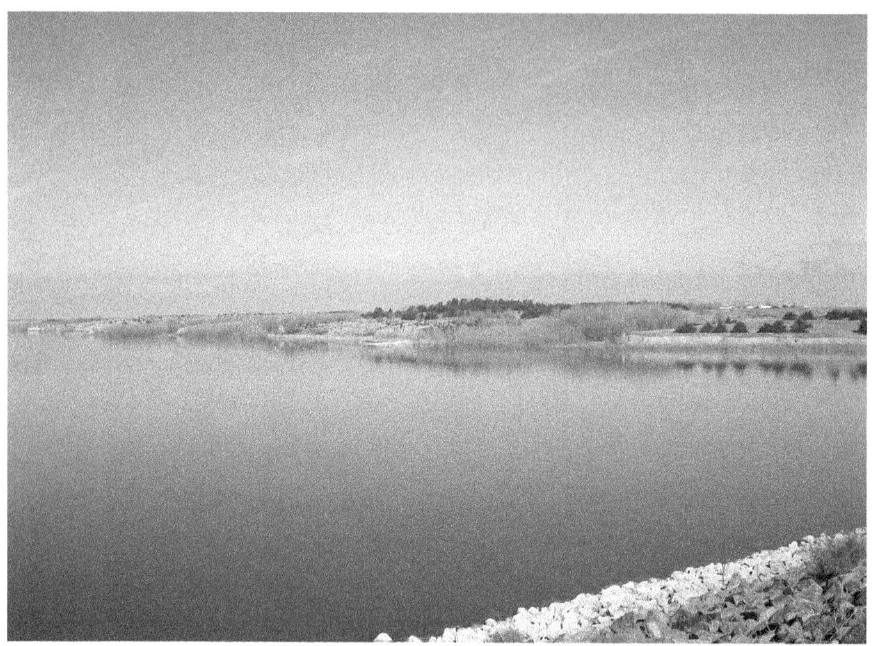

Photo of the Swanson Reservoir taken from the Trenton Dam. *Author's collection.*

in earnest. Due to the effect of these reservoirs and irrigation and upstream uses, the river's flow rates have now decreased. As a result, damaging floods have not occurred since 1960.

After construction, many believed that the new source of crop irrigation provided a desirable balance between crop and livestock production. Yields improved for principal crops such as corn, wheat, alfalfa hay and sorghum. These areas were also developed as convenient places for enjoying the natural beauty of the region. Jobs were created for those who serve the fishermen and tourists. Reservoirs provided thousands of people with the opportunity to enjoy water-oriented sports such as boating, skiing, swimming, fishing, camping and waterfowl hunting. They also provided excellent angling for bass, catfish, crappie, pike, drum, walleye and other common warm-water species. Hunters find that the numerous habitats developed at each location provide food and cover for pheasant, quail, small fur-bearing animals and mule and whitetail deer.

Life along the Republican returned to the normal ebb and flow of daily work and play. Nature worked a slow magic on the region as the months and years passed. The sand and debris were dried by the hot winds of summer. Seeds of every variety blew into the area, and soon a forest of cottonwoods and other hardy trees lined the river. Eroded fields were fertilized and the ground amended until crops could once again be planted. Within thirty years, it became harder and harder to find any traces of the flood.

Area residents began to reap the benefits from recreation areas created by the dams erected to hold back the Republican. Farmers dreamed of bigger and better farms, thanks to the accessibility of new sources of irrigation. Building began with the confidence that flooding could not happen again along the subdued river. Agencies formed in all three states to control the river and its tributaries.

Chapter 13

What Remains for the Republican

Dams and reservoirs soon sliced the Republican into small pieces, like a snake under the hoe of an angry housewife. People relaxed, considering it once again a harmless stream. Residents felt they held the upper hand in their battle to control flooding. The Republican not only became the property of the United States government but also now answers to the three state governments through which it flows and a plethora of local boards and management agencies.

Within this microcosm of regulations about its use, the water in the Republican became a prime source for crop irrigation. A 1995 survey done by the Nebraska Natural Resource Commission revealed that 72 percent of the river's surface water was diverted for irrigation, 15 percent had evaporated while stored in reservoirs and the small remainder was used for public water supplies, both commercial and domestic; mining; and livestock production.

In addition to use of the surface water in the river, farmers tapped groundwater feeding the Republican for irrigation in the postwar years. Irrigated acres, according to the Republican River Basin Water and Drought Portal, increased from slightly over thirty thousand to almost 3 million in the year 2000. According to the Republican River Rapid Watershed Assessment, there are now over twelve thousand irrigation wells in the Republican River Basin.

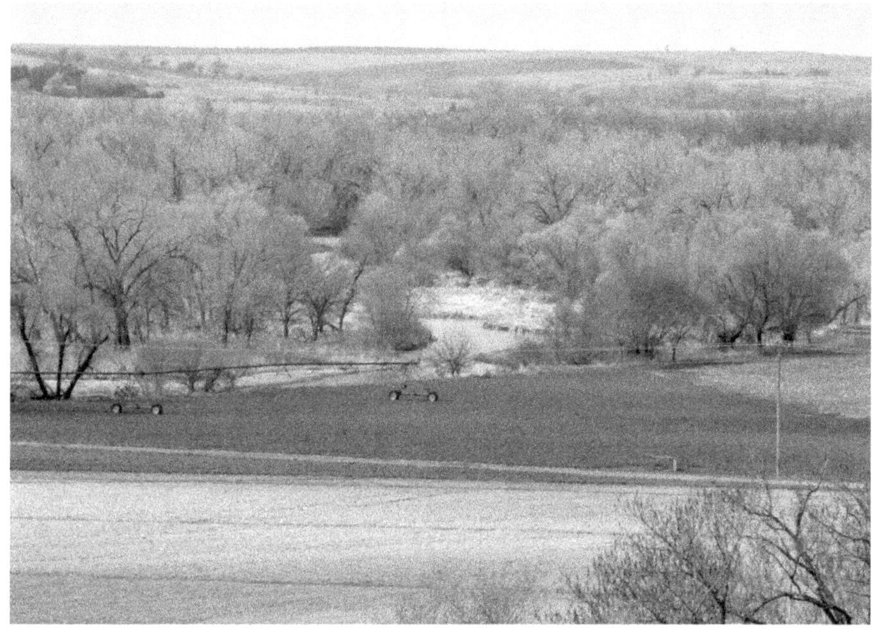

Irrigated fields near the Republican River. *Author's collection.*

Other changes introduced to the area included the construction of feedlot complexes for cattle, ethanol plants for fuel production and the introduction of several nonnative, invasive species of plants and animals to the Republican Valley. All of these changes depleted the river. The use of so much groundwater caused significant changes in the way water returned to the streams that fed the Republican, and water levels began to drop. Drought conditions in the valley compounded these problems, with the river literally drying up in many places near its headwaters. According to the University of Nebraska's drought information website, the Republican River in Hitchcock County stopped flowing and stood completely dry on July 25, 2005.

The compacts between the states eroded into controversy in the 1980s when Kansas expressed concern that Nebraska was using too much of the groundwater that belonged to Kansas. Following motions and countermotions taken before the United States Supreme Court, it was determined that Colorado also used more than its share of the water, depleting flow into the Republican at its headwaters. The court recommended that the states negotiate an agreement to fairly distribute the groundwater.

In 2004, the Republican River Water Conservation District (RRWCD) formed in Colorado to create local involvement in the new agreement reached between the three states. According to the district's website, stream flows are monitored on the Republican River at the Colorado-Nebraska state line; on the Arikaree River at Haigler, Nebraska; and on the South Fork of the Republican at Benkelman, Nebraska.

To reduce the depletion of both ground and surface water, a landowner's well could be voluntarily retired and the land returned to grassland. This land, held in the Conservation Reserve Enhancement Program (CREP) for a period of fifteen years, would, according to the program's website, "reduce irrigation water use, improve water quality, and enhance wildlife habitat through establishment of vegetative cover. Saving water will also replenish streams, rivers and reservoirs and enhance wildlife." No new irrigated land has gone into production in Nebraska's Natural Resource District since 2004.

Under the agreement, groundwater would also be pumped into the Republican to repay Kansas for water owed under the amended compact. To comply with this portion of the agreement, a Compact Compliance Pipeline (CCP) was constructed. According to the RRWCD's website:

> *The CCP is a $71 million project that is intended to deliver groundwater from wells located north of Laird, Colorado, to the North Fork of the Republican River a short distance upstream from the stream flow gage at the Colorado/Nebraska State line to offset stream depletions to comply with Colorado's Compact allocations. The December 2002 Final Settlement Stipulation between the States of Kansas, Nebraska, and Colorado to resolve pending litigation in the U.S. Supreme Court imposed a moratorium on the construction of new wells and groundwater development, but included an exception for wells associated with an augmentation plan that are acquired by a State for the purpose of offsetting stream depletions in order to comply with its Compact allocations.*

The pipeline started delivering water to the North Fork of the Republican River in January 2014.

According to the *Lincoln Journal Star*, in 2007, Nebraska began paying to remove invasive trees and vegetation from the Republican River to increase stream flow into Kansas. The unicameral voted to continue this project for a total of four years. Organizations such as the Natural Resource District in Nebraska have continued the practice of removing Russian olive trees and planting over fifty thousand other trees beneficial in preventing soil erosion and runoff into the Republican River.

To further comply with the new agreement, Colorado state officials began draining Bonny Reservoir near Idalia in late 2011. In 2012, a grass fire in

February destroyed much of the park. In March 2012, the last of the water in the reservoir, already very low from drought conditions in the area, made its way back into the river. Yuma County, Colorado, began negotiations with the State of Colorado and the Bureau of Reclamation to take control of the reservoir land now designated as a state wildlife area. Included in the property discussion is a $9 million visitors' center in a serious state of disrepair.

The Republican River is now at the center of a new controversy, the problem of water management in the High Plains. As stated in a recent report on the need for hydrologic observatories in the area:

> *The sustainability of water resources in the High Plains aquifer is a key issue for the nation. The High Plains aquifer is the largest ground-water system in North America, providing about 30 percent of the ground water used for irrigation in the United States. The region overlying the aquifer is one of the most important agricultural areas in the United States, comprising approximately 20 percent of the nation's irrigated land. Consumption of ground water in the aquifer, primarily for irrigation use, at a faster rate than capture of recharge has caused declines in water levels across large portions of the area. In addition, these declines have caused substantial long-term decreases in stream flow in many areas.*

A variety of agencies now struggle with many important questions vital to determining the future of life along the Republican. Studies are ongoing to determine if global climate change is a factor in the Republican's reduced flow. Additional studies examine the environmental impacts the river sustains due to increased population, increased irrigation and increased use of a variety of chemicals for agricultural and industrial use. Important questions are being raised about the sustainability of life along the Republican as the cycles of drought and wind further deplete the resources in the area. The natural cycles of life along the river are now under close scrutiny. As stated in a report by Derrel Martin, professor at the University of Nebraska–Lincoln, "Water use can be viewed at several scales and each perspective offers a different conclusion regarding water balances and the impact of man's activity. It is essential to consider these perspectives in managing water and to clearly define the perspective to avoid misunderstanding and false expectations." Positive signs emerged in an agreement reached on October 22, 2014. According to a *McCook Gazette* article dated October 23, agreements between Colorado, Kansas and Nebraska indicated that "the ability of the states to work together in resolving these issues is a significant step forward."

The earth is resilient, as are the people who inhabit the Republican Valley. Occasionally, the land gives up a reminder of the 1935 flood. Farmers will find a car body or a tangle of fence wire when they are working the ground. Some excavated sand pits still reveal traces of 1935 cornfields, buried under sand by the flood's deposits.

Many pause each year on Memorial Day to remember those who lost their lives when the air blew thick with dust for days and then, without warning, entire families drowned before morning. The *Omaha World Herald* stated in a special issue in June 1935 that the Republican Valley suffered one of the greatest shocks in its history. But it was not the first time the people of the area had been faced with seemingly insurmountable problems and circumstances. The *Herald* issued a challenge to turn the tragedy into an opportunity for all men and women.

Today, residents look back and marvel at the stamina, courage and resourcefulness of those who quietly accepted the challenge and went to work. They refused to give up and rebuilt even stronger communities than existed before the disaster. At the Thompson ranch in Colorado, Walt Thompson began to plan how he would rebuild his place even before he was rescued from the roof of his house during the flood. He and his family survived the flood, and they were all he needed to begin again. With the help of a banker who loaned money at no interest, as well as friends and neighbors who helped when they could, the ranch recovered, and the family prospered.

The flood became a marker in time. People told the stories of their lives, stating that the event either happened before or after the flood. In a letter dated June 16, 1935, Lois Ruplinger of Orleans, Nebraska, wrote, "We are a gritty people for the most part out here and already new hope has sprung to life and men and women are working as they never worked before." Regina Whipple Oldham remembered going out to view the sandy desert where the river once flowed shortly after the flood. She found an iris blooming amid the devastation. When she told her mother about the flower, her mother told her if the iris could take root and bloom, she should live by its example and take courage and go on living and blooming, too.

The Republican still meanders through the valley, now hemmed in by dams and reservoirs, lined with trees and crisscrossed with bridges. It has returned to its quiet ways, a gentle giant sleeping on the prairie. Will it waken again as it did in 1935? Will it survive the effects of reduced groundwater, invasive vegetation and the bickering of agencies fighting over one of the area's most precious resources, its water? The next chapter in the Republican River story is being written today by the actions taken by those who live along its banks, those who control the rights to its waters and those who govern the land through which it flows.

Chapter Notes

Introduction

Stories about the Miller family are found in multiple newspaper accounts and other articles about the flood. As with any retelling of a dramatic story from many sources, the details vary. My story is a compilation of the events as described in *Bluff to Bluff*, *Bluff to Bluff Too* and the May 28, 2010 edition of the *McCook Daily Gazette*.

Chapter 1

Over the past four years, I have spoken to people in communities up and down the Republican. I am grateful to them for the stories they shared with me. I hope that I have reported them accurately. I did my best to combine the memories of so many into this small account of a major event in their lives.

Citizens in each community along the river shared their memories with me. Many were often surprised to learn, even after all these years, that similar events had taken place in other communities in adjoining states during the flood.

In addition to cited sources, I received a wealth of information from a conversation with Raymond Borchers, author of *High Water Mark*. After Raymond's retirement from the University of Nebraska–Lincoln, he spent many hours researching the flood. In addition to his book, he compiled a video account of his trip along the Republican. He shared his story and his memoirs of his search for the true account of the flood. Two of the items on his "bucket list" were writing an account of the flood and researching and writing about George Armstrong Custer. To his credit, Borchers accomplished both tasks!

The director of the museum in Wray, Colorado, Ardith Hendrix, provided me with the proclamation on the day of prayer in Colorado in 1935.

Chapter 2

Exposed by wind and water, "giant" bones continue to be found along the broken edges of hills near the river today. Now recognized as the leg bones of great mastodons, they often measure over three feet in length. An excellent example, from a discovery made near Trenton, Nebraska, can be found at the University of Nebraska State Museum in Lincoln at www.museum.unl.edu/research/vertpaleo/stego.html.

Julene Bair, a regional author and steward of the environment, also provided information through e-mail and conversation. She is a local expert on both the Native American culture of the area and the environmental impacts of overuse of resources in the High Plains. For a broader, more in-depth treatment of these issues and the modern-day use of the Ogallala Aquifer, see Julene's book *The Ogallala Road*, published by Viking Press in 2014.

"Prehistory and Environment in the Central Great Plains" by Waldo R. Wedel, *Transactions of the Academy of Science* (1903–) 50, no. 1 (June 1947): 1–18. Published by the Kansas Academy of Science. http://www.jstor.org/stable/3625653.

Report by Captain J.C. Fremont titled "Narrative of the Exploring Expedition to the Rocky Mountains in 1842 and to Oregon & North Carolina in the Years 1843–44," published in 1845 in Washington, D.C., by Blair and Rives Printers.

Data on the geology of the river and surrounding area came from reports compiled by the United States Geological Survey and United States Bureau of Reclamation, including websites and reports cited in the bibliography.

http://digitalcommons.unl.edu/cgi/viewcontent.cgi?article=1000&context=natlpark.

http://www.umanitoba.ca/faculties/arts/anthropology/manarchnet/chronology/paleoindian/folsom.html.

http://www.usbr.gov/projects//ImageServer?imgName=Doc_1261497518250.pdf.

Chapter 3

Much of the information on the way of life in the early 1930s preceding the flood came from personal interviews and local histories of families who lived in the area at the time. Many of these families continue to make their homes in the valley. They have found not only a place to make a living but also a place to make a life. Additional information was found at these websites:

http://digitalcommons.unl.edu/cgi/viewcontent.cgi?article=1374&context=greatplainsquarterly.
http://www.ianrpubs.unl.edu/live/g1551/build/g1551.pdf.

Chapter 4

Nebraska livestock could not be identified after the flood, as branding laws did not go into effect in the state until 1938. Still, farmers knew their animals just as they knew their family members. Newspapers and family histories record many joyous reunions that took place when a farm family found their milk cows or horses. Some animals responded to their owners' voices and came running to greet them.

Chapter 5

Research on the flood led me to the Corliss Ranch. The family showed me a field that, despite it being more than seventy-five years since the flood, has never regained the productivity lost when the fertile topsoil went down the Republican on May 30, 1935.

Curious about Fitzpatrick's theory, I contacted the United States Geological Survey in Colorado and received this reply from James Dewey:

> *The observations strike me as most consistent with the crack being the result of erosion by flood water—the report of gurgling water at depth within the crack seems to me to be a particularly strong indication of erosion by flood water, with the temporary stream that caused the erosion still carrying water from the saturated ground. Another possibility would be some kind of shallow failure of the ground, some kind of lateral earth flow, caused by the saturation of the soil, although I wouldn't necessarily expect gurgling water in such a situation. In the second case, one would expect to see that the crack occurred in an area with slopes, at the top of a slope.*
>
> *The observations aren't consistent with the crack representing a tectonic fault associated with an earthquake. An earthquake large enough to produce dramatic surface faulting would be felt over all of Colorado east*

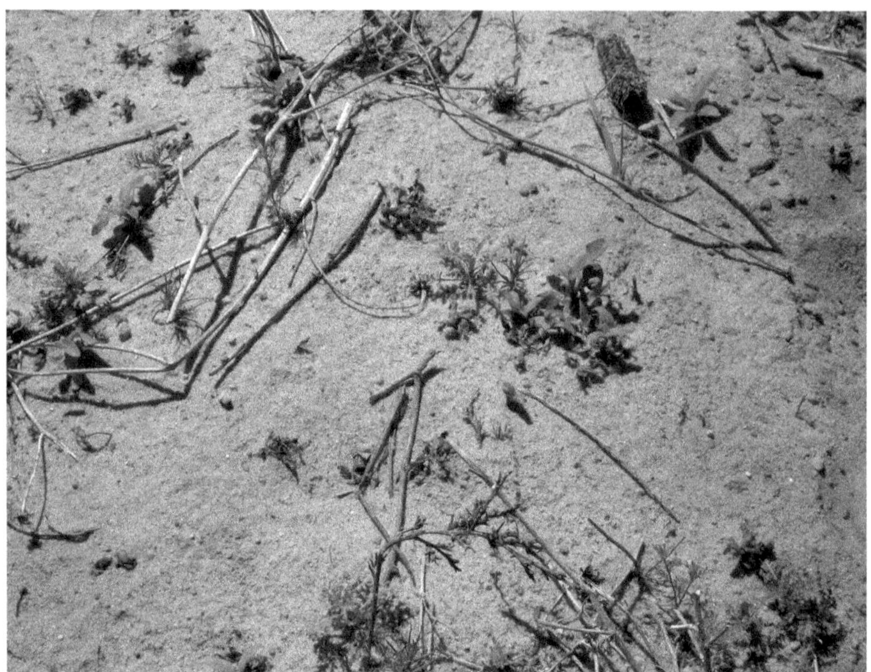

The soil on some fields of the Corliss Ranch still shows effects of the 1935 flood. *Author's collection.*

> *of the mountains and western Kansas and Nebraska, and there would be no uncertainty among people near the epicenter that the vibrations they were feeling were caused by an earthquake—they would have felt such an earthquake very strongly, many objects would have been thrown from shelves, and there would be damage to buildings. However, although I don't share Fitzpatrick's conviction that the crack may have been caused by an earthquake, I was certainly interested to read the account. What a harrowing experience for those in the area!*

Frankie Gesner, one of the Seibert flood victims, was carried all the way to McCook, where her body was misidentified and buried as that of Delores Wallace. Delores's body was later located and positively identified. Frankie's mother heard of the event and contacted the Red Willow County coroner. She was able to identify the body of her daughter by examining locks of her hair, cloth from her blouse and her daughter's wedding ring. It was months later before Frankie's body was finally returned to her mother for burial in March 1936.

Chapter 7

The story of the Mollisons' dog leading Rogers to safety made all the local papers. Mollison leased the ground to a local hunter, Dr. F.S. Bennell, who served as one of two physicians in the area at the time. He visited the farm frequently and knew Rogers and the Mollisons' shepherd dog well. The dog disappeared from the farm a few months after the flood. Both the Mollison family and Dr. Bennell mourned the loss of the dog, a very intelligent animal.

One evening about a year after the flood, Dr. Bennell and his wife attended a basketball game in Palisade, Nebraska, where they saw a similar-looking dog on the school grounds. The dog appeared to be in terrible condition, with his feet worn down and sore. He also appeared to be lost. Dr. Bennell suspected that the dog belonged to Mollison. He knew of a trick the dog performed many times when he visited the farm. After saying, "Come on, roll over," the dog would roll over very quickly in a special way. He approached the dog and gave the command. The dog performed the trick "quick as scat" and jumped into the doctor's arms, showing that he remembered him.

Dr. Bennell, overjoyed to have found the animal, and afraid of losing him if he attended the game, loaded the dog in the car and returned to Trenton. He drove to Guy Mollison's barbershop, where he entered the shop and told him he had found a dog Mollison might like. Guy said he once owned a dog and did not want another. Dr. Bennell insisted he come out to his car to look at the dog and instructed his wife to open the car door.

The dog raced to the door of the shop. He seemed quite familiar with the place and rushed in to greet all his old friends. Mollison still doubted this was his dog. Dr. Bennell insisted Mollison try the familiar trick. Guy told the dog to roll over. The dog performed the trick and then leapt into Guy's arms, overjoyed to be home.

The dog's disappearance caused much speculation. Dr. Bennell guessed someone stole the dog. The condition of the dog's feet indicated that he had spent days on the road walking home. The dog remained safely with the Mollisons for the remainder of his long life.

Chapter 8

The river wreaked a vicious revenge on Bob French's efforts to rescue others. He endured years of suffering, as the filthy water compromised his diabetic condition, leading to an early death at the age of thirty-eight. Bob, like many others rescued that day, suffered because of the poisons dealt out in the evil waves. After being rescued, most people who had been in the floodwater took a potion with a basis of cream or milk. The mixture made them vomit up the filthy water and the poisons it contained. Many other flood victims like Bob suffered for years from their experiences.

Chapter 9

Four years after the flood, a dream revealed the location of Reverend Bragg's body. Bee James, a Culbertson resident, woke from a vivid dream and knew exactly where to find Bragg. James immediately got out of bed and sharpened his spade. He went to the place where the Bragg house still stood to confirm his vision. He started to dig in the area revealed in his dream and found the skull of Bragg within minutes. Positive identification came quickly due to both Bragg's dental work and his watch, found at the same location. The watch had stopped at 6:45 p.m., the exact time the flood had coursed through his home. Bee reported that he did not know why he had the dream. He told friends the dream left him with such a strong feeling about the location of the body that he just woke and felt the need to act.

Information on flow rates on the Republican came from http://water.usgs.gov/edu/measureflow.html.

Chapter 10

Forrest Stewart heard about a steam engine used on a bridge construction job during the flood near Clay Center. His father told him the floodwaters swallowed it up during the flooding. This story remained a myth in his family until November 2005, when thirty volunteers dug down twenty-five feet and excavated the lost treasure.

http://cjonline.com/stories/121105/mid_bigdig.shtml.
http://steamtraction.farmcollector.com/steam-engines/saved-from-the-republican.aspx.

Chapter 12

A great effort has been made to restore the Neiswanger flood markers to their original condition. Citizens from many communities, including Virginia Roberts from Cambridge, Nebraska, and Bill Baumbach of Indianola, Nebraska, worked very hard to preserve these testaments to the power of the 1935 flood. Virginia has also written a small book about Mr. Neiswanger and his efforts to preserve Nebraska history. It is available at the Cambridge Museum.

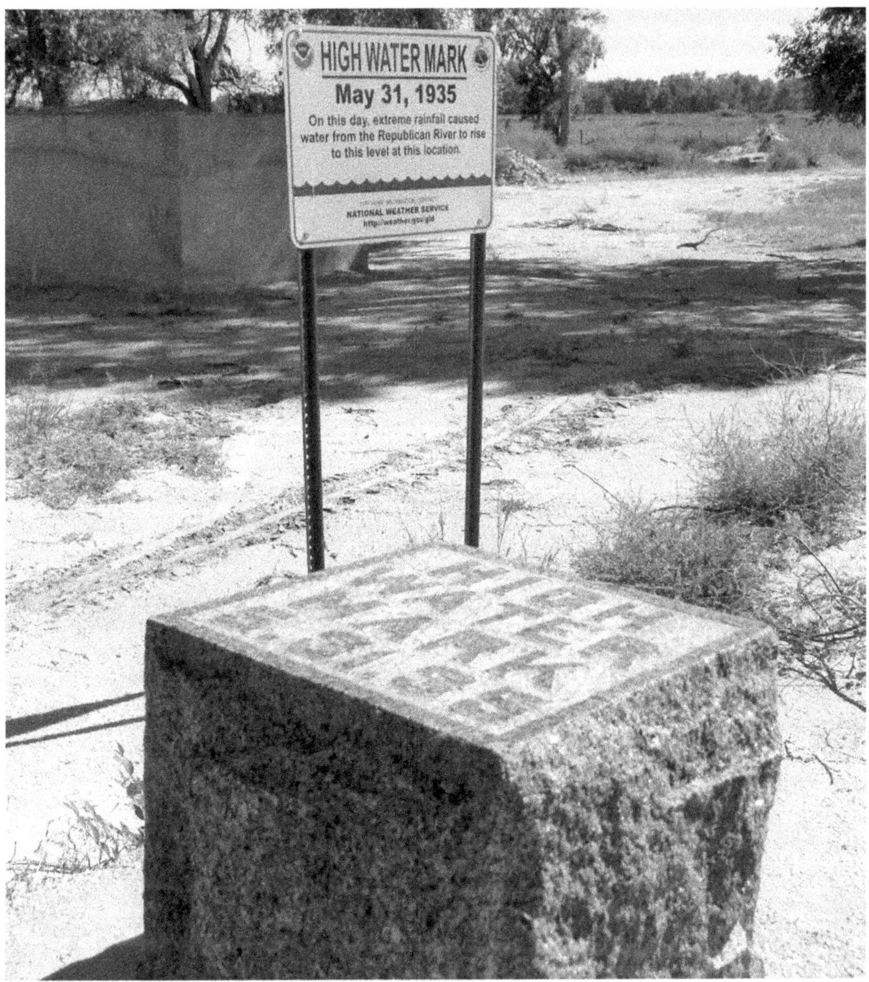

The Neiswanger high-water mark pictured with a marker placed by the Goodland, Kansas National Weather Service in the background. *National Weather Service.*

The National Weather Service also placed signs at each known Neiswanger stone location to highlight the 1935 high-water marks. More information can be found on its website: www.crh.noaa.gov/gld/?n=1935flood-hwmarks.

Additional Resources

http://www.rrbdp.org/basin_water.html.

http://www.usbr.gov/projects/ImageServer?imgName=Doc_1261497518250.pdf.

Chapter 13

Data came from the following resources:

http://dnr.ne.gov.
http://journalstar.com/news/local/govt-and-politics/bill-would-continue-paying-to-clear-rivers/article_3b8baa4c-9fa3-5f85-b6a4-e3fe841f17a2.html.
http://watercenter.unl.edu/Downloads/ResearchInBrief/MartinWaterUse.pdf.
http://water.unl.edu/drought/whatisdrought.
http://www.fsa.usda.gov/FSA/newsReleases?area=newsroom&subject=landing&topic=pfs&newstype=prfactsheet&type=detail&item=pf_20110920_consv_en_platte.html.
http://www.republicanriver.com/Home/tabid/72/Default.aspx.
http://www.usbr.gov/projects/ImageServer?imgName=Doc_1261497518250.pdf.

Bibliography

Cambridge Museum
612 Penn Street
Cambridge, Nebraska 69022

Cloud County Historical Museum
Marilyn Johnston
635 Broadway
Concordia, Kansas 66901

Shirley Coupal
Interviews with family members Margaret LaBarge Foddrill, Betty Carver and Levi Coupal.

High Plains Historical Society
421 Norris Avenue
McCook, NE 69001

Museum of the High Plains
Russ Dowling
413 Norris Avenue
McCook, NE 69001

Nebraska Historical Society (with special thanks to Linda Hein)
P.O. Box 8255
1500 R Street
Lincoln, NE 68501

Nebraska Prairie Museum
North Highway 183
Holdrege, NE 68949-0164

Republican River Riparian and Restoration Partners
Ted Tietjen
Box 849
Grant, NE 69140

Republican River Water Conservation District
410 Main Street, Suite 8
Wray, CO 80758

Wilmot Publishing Ventures
Marlene Harvey Wilmot
2625 Fifty-eighth Avenue
Greeley, CO 80634

Books and Memoirs

Bair, Julene. Interview and correspondence.

Blosser, Charles. *Why Live to Be 100 When You Can Do It in 50?* N.p., 1976.

Borchers, Raymond. *High Water Mark.* Lincoln, NE: Accent Printing, 1983.

Cheyenne County (Kansas) Historical Society. *1935 Republican River Flood.* Bird City, KS: Independent Printing, 2001.

Curtis, Carl T., and Regis Courtemanche. *Forty Years Against the Tide: A Washington Memoir.* Washington, D.C.: Regnery Gateway Inc., 1986.

Davis, Russell. "1935 Flood." Personal memoirs.

Fitzpatrick, V.S. *Back Trail Disaster.* Chicago: Adams Press, 1986.

Homm, Burdine. "Dust Storm and Flood, 1935." Personal memoirs.

Kit Carson County Cattlemen's Association. *Kit Carson County and Its Cattlemen.* N.p., 1963.

Kit Carson County History Book Committee. *History of Kit Carson County, Colorado.* Dallas, TX: Curtis Media Corporation, 1988.

Knuth, Nancy. The historical research of Nancy Knuth of Oxford, Nebraska, including the oral history reports she transcribed as part of her own project to document the flood.

Leiszler, Shirley. Clifton 125th/150th Anniversary Book.

Mann, Josephine Krug. "The 1935 Flood." Personal memoirs.

Oxford Centennial Committee. *Four Score and Seven Years*. Oxford, NE: Oxford Centennial Committee, 1968.

Pieper, Bernice. "The Josiah Harding Family." Personal memoirs.

Purvis, Tom, trans. Interview with Ernest Purvis, 2011.

Roberts, Virginia, and Jean Smith. "The Neiswanger Monuments." Personal memoirs.

Sherk, Mary L., comp. *Swept Away*. Broomfield, CO: Prairie Print, 1989.

Weisen, Dennis. The stories of Dennis Weisen from the McCoy Ranch in eastern Colorado.

Western Cartographers. *Atlas of Hitchcock County in Nebraska*. South Sioux City, NE: Western Cartographers, 1980.

Wilmot, Marlene Harvey. *Bluff-to-Bluff: The 1935 Republican Valley Flood*. Greeley, CO: Wilmot Ventures, 1995.

Newspapers of Colorado, Kansas and Nebraska

Benkelman Post and News-Chronicle. June 7, 1935.

Burlington Record. "Millennium Memories." December 30, 2004.

Cambridge Clarion. June 6, 1935.

———. June 13, 1935.

———. January 23, 1936.

———. April 13, 1939.

Clay Center Dispatch. June 4, 1935.

———. June 10, 1935.

———. November 30, 2005.

Colby Free Press. June 5, 1935.

———. June 12, 1935.

Concordia Blade-Empire. June 1, 1935.

———. June 7, 1985.

Emporia Gazette. June 3, 1935.

Franklin Sentinel. June 6, 1935.

Guide Rock Signal. June 6, 1935.

Haigler News. June 13, 1935.

Harlan County Journal. August 8, 1935.

Junction City Union. June 3, 1935.

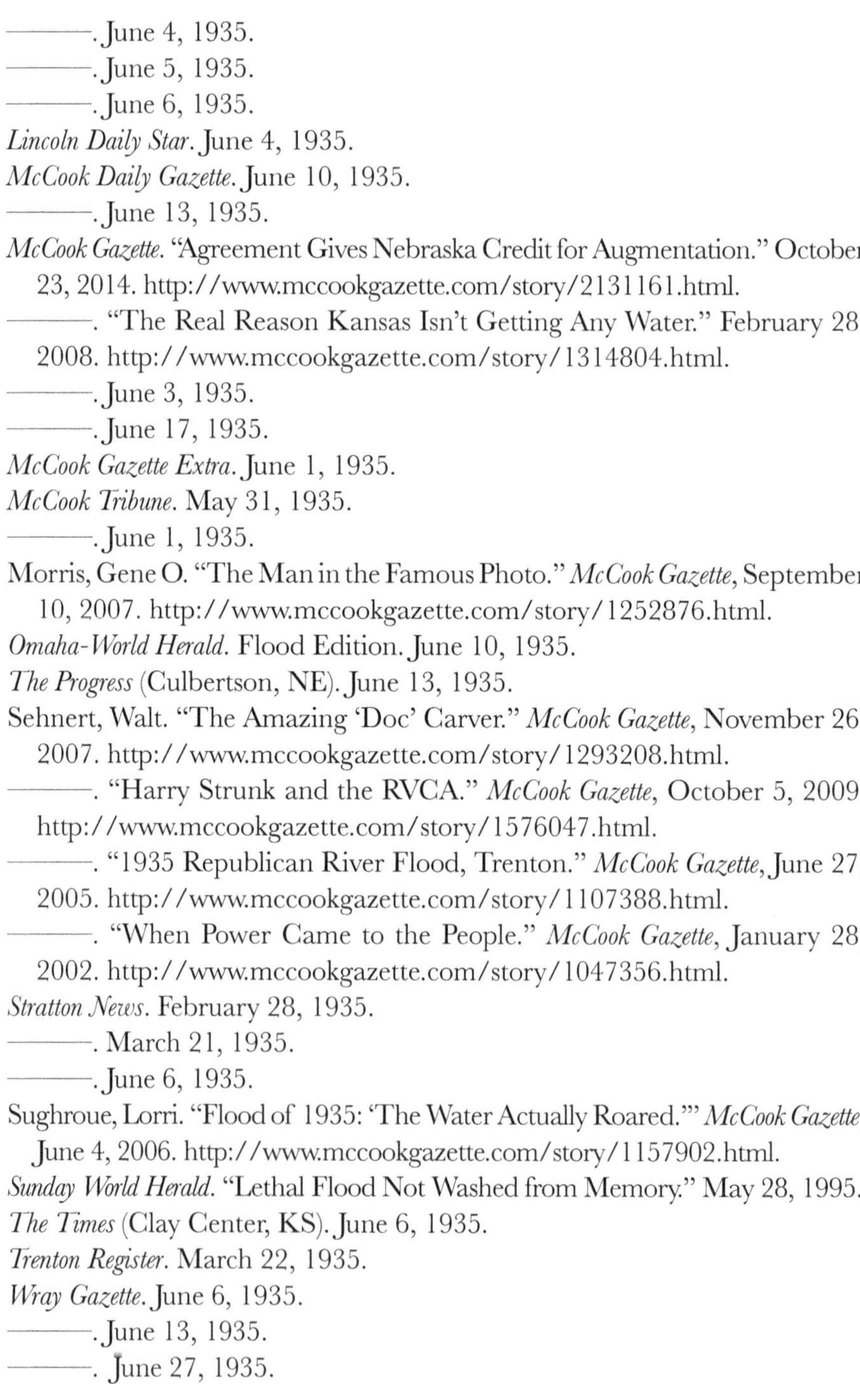

———. June 4, 1935.
———. June 5, 1935.
———. June 6, 1935.
Lincoln Daily Star. June 4, 1935.
McCook Daily Gazette. June 10, 1935.
———. June 13, 1935.
McCook Gazette. "Agreement Gives Nebraska Credit for Augmentation." October 23, 2014. http://www.mccookgazette.com/story/2131161.html.
———. "The Real Reason Kansas Isn't Getting Any Water." February 28, 2008. http://www.mccookgazette.com/story/1314804.html.
———. June 3, 1935.
———. June 17, 1935.
McCook Gazette Extra. June 1, 1935.
McCook Tribune. May 31, 1935.
———. June 1, 1935.
Morris, Gene O. "The Man in the Famous Photo." *McCook Gazette*, September 10, 2007. http://www.mccookgazette.com/story/1252876.html.
Omaha-World Herald. Flood Edition. June 10, 1935.
The Progress (Culbertson, NE). June 13, 1935.
Sehnert, Walt. "The Amazing 'Doc' Carver." *McCook Gazette*, November 26, 2007. http://www.mccookgazette.com/story/1293208.html.
———. "Harry Strunk and the RVCA." *McCook Gazette*, October 5, 2009. http://www.mccookgazette.com/story/1576047.html.
———. "1935 Republican River Flood, Trenton." *McCook Gazette*, June 27, 2005. http://www.mccookgazette.com/story/1107388.html.
———. "When Power Came to the People." *McCook Gazette*, January 28, 2002. http://www.mccookgazette.com/story/1047356.html.
Stratton News. February 28, 1935.
———. March 21, 1935.
———. June 6, 1935.
Sughroue, Lorri. "Flood of 1935: 'The Water Actually Roared.'" *McCook Gazette*, June 4, 2006. http://www.mccookgazette.com/story/1157902.html.
Sunday World Herald. "Lethal Flood Not Washed from Memory." May 28, 1995.
The Times (Clay Center, KS). June 6, 1935.
Trenton Register. March 22, 1935.
Wray Gazette. June 6, 1935.
———. June 13, 1935.
———. June 27, 1935.

Websites and Other Sources

Diffendal, Robert F., et al. "Field Guide to the Geology of the Harlan County Lake Area, Harlan County, Nebraska: With a History of Events Leading to Construction of Harlan County Dam." http://digitalcommons.unl.edu/cgi/viewcontent.cgi?article=1078&context=natrespapers.

Follansbee, Robert, and J.B. Spiegel. "Flood on Republican and Kansas Rivers, May and June 1935." http://pubs.usgs.gov/wsp/0796b/report.pdf.

MartinCassidy.com. "Josiah and His Family." http://www.martincassidy.com/graham/hardingB.html.

McGuinness, Reverend Monsignor E.J., PhD. "Nebraska's Twin Disasters." *Extension Magazine* (August 1935).

National Weather Service. "Republican River Flood of May 30, 1935." http://www.crh.noaa.gov/gld/?n=1935flood.

Nebraska State Historical Society. "The Republican River Flood of 1935." http://www.nebraskahistory.org/publish/markers/texts/republican_river_flood_1935.htm.

Reeser, Rick. Interview with Lester Confer. December 12, 2009.

RootsWeb. "The Flood of 1935 of the Republican River: Memories of Louis F. Wolf." http://www.rootsweb.ancestry.com/~neredwil/35flood.htm.

Spencer, Warren. "Great Flood of 1935. " *Nebraskaland*, June 1971.

Upper Republican River Natural Resources District. "Republican River Basic Fact Sheet." http://www.urnrd.org/BasinWideFactSheet2012%20%283%29.pdf.

U.S. Department of the Interior, Bureau of Reclamation. "Bostwick Division." http://www.usbr.gov/projects/ImageServer?imgName=Doc_1261497518250.pdf.

U.S. Geological Survey. "Bulletin 137." http://pubs.usgs.gov/bul/0137/report.pdf.

Waymarking.com. "Mystery of Standing Rock—Steedman, MO." http://www.waymarking.com/waymarks/WM557C.

About the Author

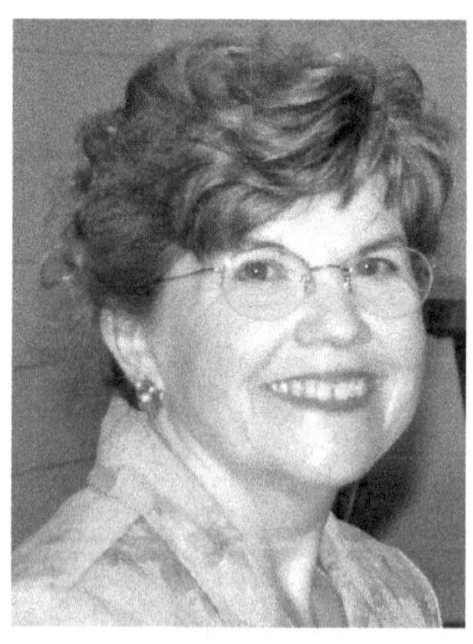

Joy Hayden has always had a love for history and strong ties to the High Plains region. As a girl, she was fascinated by the stories her grandparents told about their family history. When she married into a family of farmers and ranchers, she soon learned to love both the land and the stories her husband's family told about their struggle to survive through droughts, floods and the challenges of life close to nature. Her commitment to the preservation of these stories is demonstrated by her active participation in the Daughters of the American Revolution, her membership in her local historical society and the interest she has in local historical events. One day several years ago, she was cleaning out a file cabinet and found a copy of the Follansbee and Spiegel report on the 1935 Republican River flood. Curiosity about the event evolved into a quest to preserve a story that was quickly fading from public memory. She has spent many years compiling the history of the flood, meeting with survivors and traveling along the river to document this important chapter in the Republican River's history.

www.ingramcontent.com/pod-product-compliance
Lightning Source LLC
LaVergne TN
LVHW052340100826
845147LV00021B/1135

* 9 7 8 1 6 2 6 1 9 8 5 5 5 *